PORPHYRY THE PHILOSOPHER

INTRODUCTION TO THE TETRABIBLOS

AND

SERAPIO OF ALEXANDRIA

ASTROLOGICAL DEFINITIONS

Translated from the Greek
by
James Herschel Holden, M.A.
Fellow of the American Federation of
Astrologers

The first edition of this translation was circulated privately in 2000, the second edition was circulated privately in 2004. The present volume contains the third edition of the translation as the first published edition.

ISBN-10: 0-86690-602-9
ISBN-13: 978-0-86690-602-9

Cover Design: Jack Cipolla

Published by:
American Federation of Astrologers, Inc.
6535 S. Rural Road
Tempe, AZ 85283

www.astrologers.com

Printed in the United States of America

TABLE OF CONTENTS

Serapio of Alexandria's Astrological Definitions

TRANSLATOR'S PREFACE

Porphyry the Philosopher was born in Tyre, Syria about 234 A.D. and studied grammar and rhetoric at Athens under Cassius Longinus (c.213-273), who changed his star pupil's name from the Syrian *Malchus* 'King' to *Porphyrios* 'Purple-clad'. In 262 Porphyry went to Rome to study Neoplatonic philosophy under the famous philosopher Plotinus (c.205-270). After several years of intense study, he became sickly and depressed, and, on Plotinus's recommendation, he moved to Sicily about 268, where he lived for five years before returning to Rome. Thereafter, he lectured on philosophy and wrote books on a variety of subjects. Both in his lectures and in his books he tried to make philosophy and other subjects intelligible to the ordinary person. He died about 304. His most famous pupil was said to be the philosopher Iamblichus (c.250-c.330).

Among Porphyry's numerous works are, a *Life of Pythagoras*, a *Life of Plotinus*, *Aids to the Study of the Intelligibles* (an account of Plotinus's philosophy), *Introduction to Aristotle's Categories* (a widely read treatise on logic), Treatises on Vegetarianism, *Against the Christians* (a detailed scholarly attack in 15 books on the Christian religion, of which only fragments have come down to us), and a book of special interest to astrologers, the *Introduction to the Tetrabiblos*.

It was apparently towards the very end of the third century that Porphyry wrote the *Introduction to the Tetrabiblos*. Julius Firmicus Maternus (fourth century) refers to Porphyry as "our Porphyry," which probably means that as a young man he had studied under him.[1] And it is possible that Porphyry's interest in astrology was what first aroused Firmicus's own interest in the subject.

In his *Introduction*, Porphyry says that Ptolemy had failed to explain some of the fundamentals of astrology adequately in his *Tetrabiblos* and had omitted some others altogether, so Porphyry proposes to supply the necessary explanations.[2] This is consistent with his efforts to make philosophy intelligible to non-philosophers. Actually, his *Introduction to the Tetrabiblos* goes further. His work is in fact a short dictionary of astrological terms. He cites Nechepso and Petosiris, Teucer of Babylon, Timaeus, Antigonus, Phnaes the Egyptian, Apollinarius, and Antiochus of Athens. He seems to have copied more than a dozen chapters of his *Introduction* more or less verbatim from Antiochus's *Treasury*, a work written a century earlier, which unfortunately has not come down to us intact.[3]

In astrological history, Porphyry is best known for the so-called "Porphyry System of Houses," a method of calculating the cusps of the intermediate houses by dividing the zodiacal arcs between the astronomical MC and the ASC and the astronomical MC and the DSC into three equal parts. This was the first quadrant system of house division and the

---

[1]See James Herschel Holden, *A History of Horoscopic Astrology* (Tempe, Az.: A.F.A., Inc., 1996), p. 63 and n. 158; 2nd ed. (Tempe, Az.: (A,F.A., Inc., 2006), pp. 65-66 and n. 158.

[2]Pingree says that despite the title and Preface the work is not a commentary on Ptolemy's *Tetrabiblos*. This is consistent with my opinion that it is actually a sort of Astrological Dictionary.

[3]See the papers by David Pingree, "Antiochus and Rhetorius" in *Classical Philology* LXXII (1977): 203-223, and "From Alexandria to Baghdâd to Byzantium. The Transmission of Astrology" in the *International Journal of the Classical Tradition* 8,1 (Summer 2001): 3-37.

third system of house division, the first being Sign-House, and the second Equal House.[1]

However, Vettius Valens (123-c.175) describes the same system in his *Anthology*, iii. 2,[2] and attributes it to an otherwise unknown astrologer named Orion. Whether Porphyry had learned of the system from Orion's book or reinvented it independently is unknown. At any rate, it now goes under Porphyry's name.

According to Pingree, Chapters 1-45 are probably part of Porphyry's original work; but Chapters 47-52 correspond verbatim to the *Paris Epitome*[3] of Antiochus's work, where they are Chapters 10, 11, 12, 14, 15, and 46. And Chapters 53-55 are spurious from an unknown source.

However, I note that Chapters 53-55 closely resemble four chapters of Sahl ibn Bishr's *The Introduction to the Science of the Judgments of the Stars*, Book I, so they are probably from a Greek text that was translated from the Arabic text of Sahl's book and mistakenly tacked on to the end of Porphyry's book by the medieval compiler.

Thus, Porphyry's *Introduction*, as it has come down to us, is a composite work probably patched together by the Byzantine astrologer Demophilus, who was active at Constantinople in the last decade of the 10th century. Some of the chapters 1-45 are very similar to chapters in the *Astrological Compendium* written by Rhetorius the Egyptian around 500 A.D.[4] These are most likely chapters from Antiochus's *Trea-*

---

[1]See my paper, "Ancient House Division," in the AFA Journal of Research, Vol. 1 (Tempe, Az.: A.F.A. Inc., 1982).
[2]Vettius Valens *Anthologiae* ed. D. Pingree (Leipzig: B. G. Teubner, 1986).
[3]Edited in CCAG VIII 3.
[4]Rhetorius the Egyptian *Astrological Compendium* trans. by James Herschel

sury, independently copied by Porphyry and two centuries later by Rhetorius.

Hephaestio of Thebes (380-after 415) in his *Apotelesmatics*[1] cites some passages from Porphyry that do not appear in our received text, so the original work was evidently somewhat more extensive than that which has come down to us. Hence, as mentioned above, the received text of Porphyry's *Introduction* does not contain all of the chapters of Porphyry's original text, but only those chapters that Demophilus could find.

The first printed edition of Porphyry's book was published by Hieronymus Wolf at Basel in 1559. There is a new modern edition by Stephen Weinstock and Emilie Boer in the *Catalogus Codicum Astrologorum Graecorum*, vol. V, Part 4, published in 1940. It is from the latter edition that I have translated Porphyry's book into English. Weinstock and Boer say that Wolf's edition was evidently made from the MS **Monacensis 59**, which they characterize as being of poor quality. (Wolf says the same thing in the preface to his edition.) The principal MSS used by Weinstock and Boer and the sigla that they adopted are these:

S Monacensis 419 saec. XIV paper ff. 157
contains Chapters 1-43 & 46-52 on ff. 108-114, and Chapters 53-55 on f. 104

D Laurentianus Plut. 28,20 saec. XIV paper ff. 267
contains Chapters 1-55 on ff. 1-18

M Marcianus 314 saec. XIV parchment ff. 286
contains Chapters 1-55 on ff. 182-195

Holden (Tempe, Az.: A.F.A., Inc.).

[1]*Apotelesmaticorum Libri Tres.* ed. by David Pingree (Leipzig: B. G. Teubner, 1973), e.g. Book ii. 10. 23-24, where some planetary positions are cited that can be dated to 5 Oct 234 (which Neugebauer thinks might be Porphyry's birth date).

L Laurentianus Plut. 28,34 saec. XI (vel X?) parchment ff. 1-170

contains Chapters 47-52 as Chapters 10-12, 14-15 & 46 of Rhetorius

H Scorialensis II. Ψ. 17 saec. XV paper
contains Chapters 49 on f. 5^v and 45-46 on ff. 38^v – 40^r

B Baroccianus Oxoniensis 94 paper ff. 189
contains Chapters 45 on f. 111^v, 35 on f. 118, a fragment of 41 on f. 114, and excerpts of Chapters 1- 44? on ff. 121^v – 125^v

The editors found MS **S** to be the best MS. MSS **D** and **M** often offer the same differences from **S**, so they are perhaps copies of a now lost MS δ. However, MSS **H** and **B** appear to be copied directly from the archetype. If I understand them

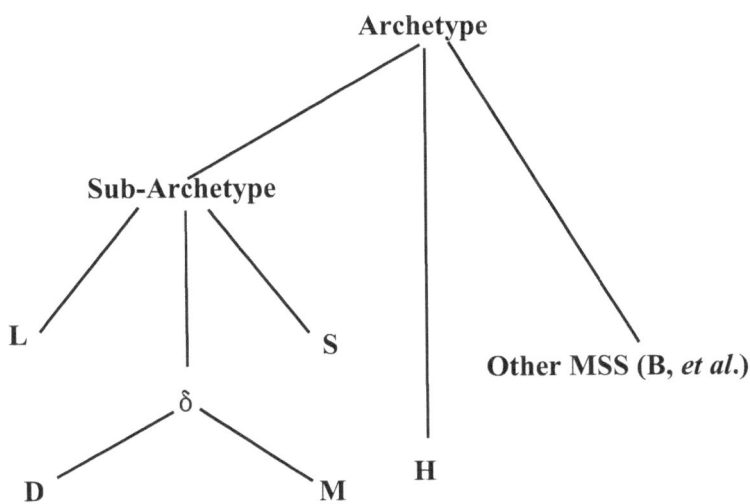

correctly, they postulate a relationship of the MSS like the above:

Despite their best editing efforts, there are a few places in the Greek text that still appear to be corrupt. These are marked by daggers or mentioned in the footnotes. I have also found it necessary to employ paraphrase more often than I usually do in translating.

James H. Holden
Phoenix, Arizona
2000

Preface to the Second Edition.

Two complete chapters and portions of three other chapters were not translated in the first edition. These have now been translated. I have also revised the entire translation, added a few footnotes, and appended a Concordance of the chapters of Antiochus's *Treasury*, Rhetorius's *Compendium of Astrology*, and the chapters of Porphyry's *Introduction* to the Preface to the First Edition.

James H. Holden
Phoenix, Arizona
December 13 2003

Preface to the Third Edition.

David Pingree's last paper on Rhetorius[1] contains some useful information on the composite text that has come down to us as Porphyry's *Introduction*. It is therefore necessary for me to revise some of my remarks in the Preface to the first Edition.

In view of Pingree's description of the sources of the several chapters, the stemma shown above would appear to refer to the descent of some of the MSS from Demophilus's compilation (the Archetype). But MS **L** actually contains chapters from a MS of Rhetorius, which Demophilus added to his copy of Porphyry's text. And I have determined that Chapters 53-55 of Porphyry's *Introduction* are in fact a version of four chapters of Sahl ibn Bishr's *The Introduction to the Science of the Judgments of the Stars*,[2] Book I; so, as mentioned previously, they are probably from a Greek text that was translated from the Arabic text of Sahl's book and mistakenly appended to Porphyry's text.

James H. Holden
Phoenix, Arizona
September 12 2007

---

[1]"From Alexandria to Baghdâd to Byzantium. The Transmission of Astrology" in the *International Journal of the Classical Tradition* 8,1 (Summer 2001): 3-37.
[2]See Sahl ibn Bishr, *The Introduction to the Science of the Judgments of the Stars*, translated by James Herschel Holden (Tempe, Az.: A.F.A., Inc., 2008).

Preface to the Published Edition.

I have made a few additions and corrections to the text of the third edition, and the opportunity has now come to publish this translation. I want to thank Kris Brandt Riske, the Executive Director of the American Federation of Astrologers, for preparing the text for publication. And I also want to thank Jack Cipolla, the AFA Operations Manager, for designing the book covers.

Also, my translation of Sahl ibn Bishr's *The Introduction to the Science of the Judgments of the Stars* was published by the A.F.A. in 2008. And my translation of Rhetorius the Egyptian's *Astrological Compendium* was published by the A.F.A. in 2009. So both of those books are now available.

James H. Holden
Phoenix, Arizona
October 15 2009

PORPHYRY THE PHILOSOPHER

INTRODUCTION TO THE ASTROLOGY OF PTOLEMY.

1. *Preface.*

Since Ptolemy treated the features of the comprehensive science of the heavenly bodies and the kinds of astrological influences that have been observed to result from it in general terms, displaying an obscure and indeed an unclear manner of speech because of the usage of old words,[1] of necessity I intend for the sake of clarity to define in advance the terms that contribute to the attainment of this [science].

And it is proper in the present work to run past the things that were distinctly stated by Ptolemy in certain places—inasmuch as they have an obvious explanation—but it seems good to us to present those things that are summarily, and at

---

[1] Ptolemy's Greek is rather crabbed and sometimes hard to understand. This may possibly indicate that his native language was Egyptian and that he had learned Greek as a second language. But Porphyry's Greek is not a model of clarity either, since he was a Syrian by birth. I have broken some of his lengthy sentences into shorter ones. And I have felt obliged to use paraphrase more often than I usually do. In general, Porphyry's language is not always easy to read.

the same time, not plainly stated, and to present them quite clearly and in a customary and befitting manner. And so, for instance, mention is made of *testimony*, and *doryphory*, and *predominance*, and *domination*, and the things we are going to include below; which, if not absolutely explained by this, will be raising new questions for the one entering upon the approaches to prognostications. Wherefore, concisely as well as clearly, following our predecessors, we are setting forth this timely *Introduction*, which ought to be easily comprehended by those uninitiated in these matters.

2. Changes Produced by the Transfers of the Sun, Moon, and Stars.[1]

The Sun was assigned to be just like a most powerful King among the celestial stars, clearly governing and arranging and setting in order the things that exist in the air, and those that exist on the earth. And the rest of the stars, presiding over the smallest change in their joint combinations with him, work with [him], or work against [him]. Naturally, therefore, the Sun is called to enumerate the seasons; since, according to its own declination, spring, and summer, and autumn, and winter hold sway; and, when they are being forecast in the seasons, hot spells and cold spells. Besides too, it is generally causative of the winds.

But to keep things in order and to create life, the Sun brings to light the disorderly and lifeless substance of life arising from incessant birth, since it has the seed of the fully completed living things, and the monthly cause of that which lies underneath. And similarly too, the things spawned by the

---

[1]This chapter is similar in content to *Tetrabiblos* i. 2, including the use of rare words, such as the verb *symmeioô* 'become less along with'.

solar warmth from the mud of the earth, and the offspring of the living things in the waters; which, in the pervading living things, from its lights, and from its skillful power of arranging, it endows with form in the arranged periods. Yet still it also naturally regulates the seeds that are seasonably concealed in the earth for sprouting.

But again, the Sun arranges all the actions appointed for the seasons, and of course they influence farmers and also those aboard ship, and the plants, along with the living things. But it leads the farmers and those aboard ship to observe the configurations of the wandering stars[1] and the fixed stars along with it for safety. It prepares those living things that are without reason[2] to stay in winter in warm dwellings and those having calm, and in summer to go to the more breathable and well-watered regions. But it also prepares the plants following it to have a sequence in the solar journey; for, according to those same seasons, they bring forth pleasant and fine-smelling flowers, and they put out buds, and they continue bringing forth all kinds of fruit.

And the Moon, being of all the stars the nearest to the earth, and blending together with her applications in their configurations, and with the magnitude of the lights of those from the same ones that are reaching into the ones there, she bears the lesser portion of the energy with respect to the Sun. And just like a Queen that is strongest in the world of the heavens, she has struck proportionately to the Sun, arranging the hours for instance—indeed the four weeks of the month—for, with the Sun running through the zodiac in its entirety in a year; the Moon, from its growing bright and taking a run, moves in nearly 29½ days from new Moon to new

---

[1]That is, the Planets.
[2]Animals.

Moon, and shows the closest relationship to the four quarters of the year.

From its first appearance down to the First Quarter, it is like Spring; and thence down to the full Moon like Summer; and down to the Second Quarter like Autumn; then, next in order down to its disappearance,[1] it is like Winter. And it does not arrange a nativity according to its creating, but it does something similar. For it influences the things subject to it, and it ripens and increases and decreases. And it corresponds to those things that are called maritime creatures—crabs, lobsters, and sea urchins, and of course the hard-shell [creatures] of the same nature as these—[that are] increasing and decreasing along with the Moon.

But again too, the plants swell and ripen with fruits and seeds from the full distribution of the wetness that is being put together along with modest warmth. But also there is made known the successive arranging of those things lying under the Moon, along with the things occurring according to nature. In women for instance, the cleansing of their menses takes place at a monthly time for the most part. And the rivers, and also the springs, and the straits increasing together and indeed emptying out together, just as is customary for them—they change with the increasing of the Moon.

And she makes 7 phases with the Sun: *crescent-shaped*, then when the Moon is 60 degrees distant from the Sun down to the following; and the quarter, when she is distant by 90 degrees; and *gibbous*, when [she is distant] 110 degrees; and full-Moon, at 180 degrees; and *second gibbous* because of the lessening of her light when her distance from the Sun goes less than 120 degrees; and the second quarter when it is

---

[1] At the time of new Moon.

90 degrees distant; and the *crescent-shape* when it is 60 degrees; and when it is less than those configurations, she goes under the Sun beams into the so-called *conjunction*.[1] And it indicates the surrounding condition of the air, for all the indications of the weather are made according to the Sun, as it draws near to each of the indicating stars.

And following after those that are defined thus, it is necessary to explain the notable risings of the planets and the distinctive combinations of the fixed stars with them, since really the *morning risings* of the planets, and their *stations*, and not in the least the *magnitudes* of the eclipses of the Lights with the concurring *conjunctions* or *full-Moons* by opposition, and in the tropical and equinoctial signs. And yet also the disposition of the heavens occurring at the time of birth, from which the whole determination is obtained for us. The most useful things occur from the natural sympathy of the signs, in which the signifying <stars> are posited in their passages, for the declaration of the way the houses are arranged and their appearances.

And from the ruler of the stars and the blending that it partakes with the others, it is possible for us to forecast about the probable good or bad things that are going to happen in addition to these, and also those of the diverse combinations of nativities.

And all of these stars rise as *morning [stars]* whenever they are distant from the conjunction in the direction preceding the Sun by 15 degrees more or less. And likewise, when the [star] of Saturn and the [star] of Jupiter and the [star] of Mars are *morning [stars]* and they are distant [from the Sun] by around 120 degrees they make their *first station* [where

---

[1]The new Moon.

5

they begin] retrograding.[1] Coming into the 6th sign; and also retrograding more, they move into the *acronychal* [position] aspecting the Sun by opposition—and at the time of its setting they rise at the beginning of night. And likewise, retrograding from the *acronychal* [position], and going into the trine following the Sun, they make their *second station*.[2] [And] again coming to the *epanaphora*[3] of the Sun and making the *vespertine setting*, they arrive at the conjunction. For the conjunction is lordly whenever it chances to be partile [conjunct] the Sun in the same sign, not being separated from it by more than 59 minutes.[4]

But the star of Mars alone also makes two other "phases" with the Sun, which those who are attentive to such things usually call "anomalies." And the first anomaly is made whenever as a *morning [star]* it goes before the Sun 82 or 90 degrees, and the second in the *vespertine setting* whenever the star is the same distance away from the Sun.[5] And always these, as is clear, make their motion less than that of the Sun.

Both the [star] of Venus and the [star] of Mercury make the things that change the livelihood of men and the things on the earth through their configuration with the Sun when they are accomplishing their daily courses rapidly or slowly. Wherefore, they also make two phases with respect to the Sun: *morning appearance*,[6] when they are *rising* before it, or

---

[1]The first station is called *static retrograde* by modern astrologers.
[2]Now termed *static direct*.
[3]That is, when it comes to the sign in the zodiac following the Sun.
[4]This seems to be an earlier version of the phase "in the heart of the Sun," where the orb is cut down to 17 or 18 minutes (the semi-diameter of the Sun).
[5]These phase differences are mentioned by Pliny, *Natural History* II, 60
[6]Here and in the latter part of the sentence I have translated *anatolê* 'rising above the horizon' as 'appearance'.

following after it by more or less than 15 degrees[1]; and *evening appearance*, when they are *setting* after it, or preceding it by less than 15 degrees, or by *setting* further after it.[2]

And when they have chanced to be within the said distance in the going before [phases], they make the *morning setting*; but in the following after [phases], they make the *evening setting*. And the [star of] Venus is stationary when its distance from the Sun comes closest to 47 degrees; but the [star of] Mercury around 23 degrees.[3] But in those following the first station, they end up being retrograde; but in those leading after the second [station], they are moving forward [again]. One must see in general, that all the stars always make a shift in the following [phase]. And only a trick of sight produced the appearance of the planets in the same degree. And the notable ones of the fixed stars, as it is stated in Ptolemy, are combined in their natures that are mixed together with regard to the planets, [and] with the natures of these they are made joint rulers and they act conformably both in the universal occurrences of the regions and in the individual peculiarities of the nativity.

---

[1]The text actually reads "when they are rising before it or rising after," but it means "rising before or following after," as I have translated it. When a planet is "rising before the Sun," it is behind it in the zodiac; hence, it is "following after the Sun."

[2]Here, where the text has "following after", I have written "setting after", since the planet must actually be "preceding the Sun", i.e being further advanced in the zodiac, in order for it to appear in the west after sunset. Either the Greek text is corrupt, or else Porphyry has simply given an incorrect definition.

[3]These values are from some pre-Ptolemaic planetary treatise. They are similar to the values 46 degrees and 22 degrees given by Pliny, NH II, 38, and are of course only approximations. For a comparison table, see O. Neugebauer, HAMA (New York; Heidelberg; Berlin: Springer Verlag, 1975. 3 vols.), Vol. 2, pp. 804-805.

3. The Configurations that the Stars Make in their High and Low Points, the Apogees, and the Perigees.

It is necessary to understand the preceding statements thoroughly in order to trace out the observed principles of astrological influences, because in their high and low points in the signs the planets make four configurations. The *first* is when going down from the highest *apside*[1] to the middle they have fallen from a high point. And the *second* is when they have gone from the middle into the lowest *apside*, returning to their *perigee*. The *third* is when from the down point they go up again to the middle, being raised up from the *perigee*. And the *fourth* is when they have come from the middle to the high point, arriving at the *apogee*.

For the stars when going down from the lofty *apside*, after becoming *synodic*[2] to the Sun, begin to move forward. And going down from the middle of the *apside*, making the *first station*, they come into the *acronychal* phase[3]; and rising up from the *perigee*, still making the *acronychal* phase, they begin to *retrograde*, and they come into the *second station*; and going up from the middle *apside* to the highest, making the *second station*, and following that, the greatest change, coming into the *synodic* relationship with the Sun, they make their *opposition*.

---

[1] Literally, a point in the orbit. Usually used only of the farthest and closest points in the orbit, but here also used of the points in between those. The "highest apside" is the apogee or the farthest point from the Earth, and the "lowest apside" is the perigee or the closest point to the Earth. Porphyry is describing the planetary motion in an epicycle.

[2] That is, "in conjunction with the Sun."

[3] The *acronychal* phase is when the planet rises when the Sun sets, i.e., when the planet is in opposition to the Sun.

4. *Diurnal and Nocturnal Stars.*

Whenever they say *diurnal stars*, they are signifying Saturn and Jupiter, declaring them to be of the Sun's sect because they do not make many settings or [other] configurations.[1] For they rejoice by day when they are effective and in the domiciles of diurnal [stars]. But when they say *nocturnal stars*, they are referring to Mars and Venus, establishing them to be of the Lunar sect. And in fact they have many configurations, often going under the setting and being obscured.[2]

However, they declare the [star] of Mercury to be *common*, for with whichever one it happens to be in configuration, to that one it is related—*oriental*, to the Sun; and *occidental*, to the Moon.

5. *The Houses which are also called Zones of the Stars.*

Houses[3] and *zones of the stars* [are what] they term the 12 twelfths of the zodiac, which they also call *signs*. Of these, the most northerly and closest to us are given to the *luminaries*—to the Moon, Cancer; and to the Sun, Leo. And [then] in order to the one nearest them, Mercury, [they give] Gemini and Virgo; after which, to Venus, Taurus and Libra; then, to Mars, Aries and Scorpio; then, to Jupiter, Sagittarius and Pisces; then to Saturn, the one farthest from us, Capricorn and Aquarius.

---

[1] Since they move more slowly than the other planets.

[2] That is, being under the Sun beams.

[3] It would be better to translate the Greek word *oikous* 'houses' as 'domiciles' (which I have done hereafter), since in modern astrology the technical term *house* refers only to the *celestial* houses. And modern astrologers speak of the *signs* of the planets. But the older writers, such as William Lilly, still used the term *houses* of the planets, despite the ambiguity.

6. *Exaltations.*

They establish [as] *exaltations* of the stars the [signs that are] trines of their diurnal domiciles and those agreeing in nature. For example, the Sun. Since Leo is its domicile, its *exaltation* is Aries, which is the trine of that [sign] and one that is quadrupedal; and the Sun has its exaltation around the 19th degree. Saturn, since its domicile is Aquarius, the *exaltation* will be Libra around the 20th degree. Jupiter, since its domicile is Pisces, its exaltation will be Cancer around the 15th degree.

For the nocturnal stars, which are of the sect of the Moon, because of the weakness of its ray, the sextile of the domicile is the *exaltation* [sign]. Let, then, the Moon's *exaltation* be the sextile of Cancer, i.e. Taurus, around the 3rd degree. The *exaltation* of Mars is the sextile of Scorpio, i.e. Capricorn, around the 28th degree. The *exaltation* of Venus is the sextile of Taurus, i.e. Pisces, around the 26th degree. But the [star] of Mercury, since it is common and its ray is dimmer because of its frequent setting, has the same domicile and *exaltation*, i.e. Virgo, around the 15th degree.[1]

And the signs opposite the *exaltations* are their *falls*, in which they have weaker powers.

7. *Co-rulers.*

They are said to be *co-ruler* with each other, whenever it is their *domicile* or their *exaltation*. And they say that some *co-rulers* are rulers of the *domiciles*, and some are rulers of

---

[1]This is an attempt to give a reason for the selection of certain signs as exaltations. However, the exaltation signs were actually designated by the Babylonians as "the secret places of the stars." And their reasons for choosing a specific sign for each planet are unknown.

the *triplicities*. For example, in the case of Aries, the *co-rulers* are the Sun and Mars; of Taurus, the Moon and Venus; of Gemini, Mercury and Saturn;[1] of Cancer, Jupiter and the Moon; of Leo, the Sun alone; of Virgo, Mercury alone; of Libra, Saturn and Venus; of Scorpio, Mars alone; of Sagittarius, Jupiter and the Sun; of Capricorn, Mars and Saturn; of Aquarius, Saturn and Mercury; of Pisces, Venus and Jupiter. And similarly too with the rest.

They say that the Sun and the Moon are *luminaries*, *Lights*, and *Kings*,[2] and *rulers of the day and the night*. In those *co-rulerships* in which the exaltation of one [of them] is not taken, they say they are *luminaries of the sect*.[3]

8. *Aspects*.

They call the mutual configurations of the stars *aspects*. And their configurations are these: the *trine* [consists] of 5 [signs],[4] whenever there are 3 signs in between the two; and the *square* of four, whenever there are two signs in between them; and the *opposition* of 7, whenever there are 5 in between; and the *sextile* of 3, whenever there is one sign in the middle of them.

And the configurations by *trine* are sympathetic and helpful, and if it is destructive,[5] it is less hurtful. The *square* is harsh and discordant and able to cause trouble if it is destruc-

---

[1]Saturn is a *co-ruler* because it is a triplicity ruler of the Air triplicity, being exalted in Libra and ruling Aquarius.

[2]Or, *rulers*.

[3]A special technical term. Usually called *Lights of the Times*.

[4]The ancients counted both ends of a sequence rather than only the intervening items and the far end as we do. Hence, from their point of view, the interval from Aries to Leo consists of 5 signs, not 4.

[5]When one or both of the end points is afflicted.

tive. The *opposition* is antagonistic, and worse if it is malefic; the *sextile* [is] feebler. It is [also] necessary to see whether the configurations are perfect according to degree[1] and not just by sign: the trine by 120 degrees, the square by 90 degrees, the sextile by 60 degrees, and the opposition by 180 degrees, for many times they are configured by sign but not by degree.[2]

9. *Dexter and Sinister Aspects.*

They say that it is a *dexter* trine or square or sextile from which the star departs, but a *sinister* one to which it comes.[3] For example, with the Sun in Leo, the trine of Aries and Leo is *dexter*, but the one to Sagittarius is *sinister*. And the *dexter* square is that of Taurus and Leo, but the one to Scorpio is *sinister*. And the *dexter* sextile is that of Gemini and Leo, but the one to Libra is *sinister*.[4]

For each star sends forth seven rays, three upwards and three downwards, and one to the opposite, of which the upward ones are *dexter* and the downward ones are *sinister*.[5]

---

[1]That is, *partile*.

[2]This refers to the original method of reckoning aspects, i.e. by sign rather than by the actual number of degrees between two planets. For example, according to the original method, every planet in Aries is square every planet in Cancer, regardless of the degrees of the planets. See the note to Chapter 10 below.

[3]*Dexter* and *sinister* are the Latin words for 'right' and 'left'. Thus, a *dexter trine* is one to the right of the starting point as seen from the center of the circle, while a *sinister trine* is one seen to the left of the starting point. In this definition, Porphyry is using the analogy of direct motion in the zodiac. A planet in Aries is moving *away* from one in Sagittarius but *towards* one in Leo.

[4]Porphyry forgets to explain that *dexter* and *sinister* refer to one end of the aspect and are reversed at the other end. For example, a planet in Leo is *dexter* trine to another planet in Aries, but at the same time the planet in Aries is *sinister* trine to the one in Leo. *Dexter* aspects had different qualities from *sinister* aspects, so the planet in Aries was affected one way by the trine, and the planet in Leo was affected in another way. This distinction has been lost in modern astrology.

[5]He is talking about aspects. The definition is correct for a point in one of the eastern quadrants. Aspects cast in the direction of the diurnal motion are *dexter* and

10. *Platic.*

They term [it] *platic* whenever the stars surpass the configuration by a degree of the equal-sided line; for example, [when] the Sun is in 19 Aries and Saturn is in 20 Libra.[1]

11. *Application and Kollêsis.*

They say that an *application* is a *kollêsis*[2] whenever they apply partilely, according for example to a configuration at some particular time, or even when they are about to come together within three degrees. It was also said if it was thus: it is a *kollêsis* whenever one star moves toward another star, the swift one moving to the slow one that is not distant more than three degrees. And in the case of the Moon, some say within thirteen degrees; that is, in both her day and night course to observe the conjunction when she applies to one of them.

---

those cast against it are *sinister*. But it is incorrect for a point in one of the western quadrants, where *dexter* aspects are downward and *sinister* aspects are upward – just the reverse of the definition.

[1] The phrase 'configuration by degree of the equal-sided line' requires some comment. The first three words refer to an aspect measured by degree rather than by sign. For example, 15 Aries is sextile 15 Gemini *by degree* (what we call *partile*) because the distance between them is exactly 60 degrees, but 5 Aries is sextile 25 Gemini *by sign*, but not *by degree* because the actual distance between them is 80 degrees. Originally, aspects were reckoned by sign (as the Hindus still reckon them), but later in the Classical Period they began to be reckoned by degree by some astrologers. The remainder of the phrase *isoskelous grammes* 'equal-sided line' apparently refers to the original concept of an aspect as being one of the equal sides of a polygon inscribed within the zodiacal circle. Hence, the whole phrase means 'the exact number of degrees in the aspect'. The term *platic* is thus applied to an aspect that is not *partile*, but only by sign.

[2] The Greek word *kollêsis* means 'gluing together' or 'sticking together—within an orb of 3 degrees, as was mentioned in Chapter 11 above. This definition is not used by modern astrologers. Since there is no modern equivalent, I have kept the Greek word in italics in the translation.

12. *Separation.*

Separation is when one star moves away from another star, and its conjunction [with it],[1] and application when it moves toward that or toward its aspect. For example, the Moon in the 20th degree of Scorpio, Saturn in the 10th degree of the same sign, and the [star] of Jupiter likewise in Scorpio in the 25th degree; it is plain that it will have its separation from Saturn, and it applies to Jupiter. Again let the Moon be in 20 Scorpio, Saturn in the 10th degree of Aquarius, [and] Jupiter in the 25th degree of Leo; therefore the Moon will have her separation from the 10th degree of Scorpio, which receives an aspect cast by Saturn by square, and she applies to the 25th of Scorpio, which receives an aspect cast by Jupiter from the previously mentioned sign.

13. *Another [Definition] of Separation.*

And they also explain separation thus: *separation* is whenever a star separates from another star—the swifter from the slower—whether from the *kollêsis* that had been made nearer, or from the application to it by aspect, whenever it begins to have more than half of the degrees of the binding[2] for the aspect.

14. *Blockade.*

They say [it is] *blockaded* whenever a star comes to be in this configuration. For example, let the Moon be in Virgo [and] Mars in Aries; Leo and Libra surround Virgo, and a ray

---

[1] Or its partile aspect with it.
[2] Cf. Rhetorius, *Astrological Compendium*, Chapter 38. "Bonding".

of Mars, which makes a trine to Leo and an opposition to Libra, the Moon is *blockaded* by malefic rays. Whenever, then, the malefics *blockade* either the Moon or the ASC, with none of the benefics having effective testimony to those that are *blockaded*, they say that the native becomes short-lived.

15. *Besieging.*

Again, they declare *besieging* to be thus: *besieging* is said whenever two stars *besiege* one in the middle, with no other interposing its ray in between; or again, a star has come into these 7 degrees, or it is going into these 7 degrees by aspect, others have cast their aspects, or the same one and one from different aspects, as was said previously.[1] And when this *besieging* happens by malefics, it is dangerous, but by benefics it is beneficent.

16. *Intervention.*

Intervention is whenever a star casts its ray into the middle degrees; for example, with the Moon being in the 10th degree of Leo and Mars in the 25th degree of Leo, then [there are] 15 degrees from the 10th degree of Leo to the 25th degree. If then the [star] of Jupiter chances to be in Aries possessing the 12th degree or more from the 10th degree to the 25th, the ray of this [star] *intervenes* in the middle degrees.[2] And in the

---

[1]This definition is not entirely clear, but it seems to define a space of 7 degrees, consisting of the degree the besieged star is in and the three degrees on either side of it. If then two stars are either within this space or casting an aspect into it, one on one side and the other on the other side, the star in the middle is said to be *besieged*. Modern astrologers would widen the surrounding space to the "orb" of the *besieged* star on either side.
[2]This also called *prohibition*.

same way too if the Moon is in the 10th degree of Leo and Jupiter [is] in the 25th, and Mars is in the 12th degree of Aries or more, as we said [before] of Jupiter, Mars *intervenes* between the Moon and Jupiter.

17. *Transfer of Nature.*

It is said to be a *transfer of nature* when one star applies to another star, and the former again to [still] another; for it conveys the power of the [first] one into the power of the other.[1]

18. *Aggregation.*

It is said to be an *aggregation* when several stars apply to one [other] star; for then [that] star takes the power of those [other stars].[2]

19. *Refrenation.*

And it is said to be a *refrenation* when the ruler of the ASC is not joined to the ruler of the house that is signifying the things of the questions.[3]

---

[1]This is somewhat like the later term, *Transfer of Light*, although the latter term requires that the intermediate star *separate* from one star and *apply immediately* to another star.

[2]This is similar to the later term, *Collection of Light*.

[3]I have substituted 'house' where the original text has 'ASC' again. And this definition seems to be incomplete from the later definition, in which one significator applies initially to the other but then turns retrograde and does not complete the application, thus being "reined in" or "restrained" as it were. And note the explicit reference to Horary Astrology!

20. *Predominating.*[1]

And the [star] that is in the tenth sign is said to be *predominant* and to prevail over the one in the fourth [sign from it], e.g. the star that chances to be in Libra is dominant over the one in Capricorn, and the one in Capricorn is dominant over the one in Aries.[2]

21. *Prevailing.*

Every star *prevails* when it is posited in a *dexter* trine or square or sextile to one on its left, for that one goes toward it. For example, one that is in Capricorn *prevails* over one in trine aspect in Taurus and one in square in Aries and one in sextile in Pisces; and it is itself *prevailed over* by one in Libra and by one in Virgo and by one in Scorpio. They say that *prevailing* is more powerful when [the planets] are in trine or square. For the *prevailing* star is thus stronger, whether it is a benefic or a malefic and also angular. For when it is a benefic, it shows a notable nativity, but a harmful [planet shows] an undistinguished [nativity]. And in general every star that is on the right[3] *prevails* over one that is on the left that is carried to it.

22. *Homorêsis.*

It is termed *homorêsis*[4] whenever stars are in the same terms, whether a *kollêsis* is being produced, or indeed when

---

[1] Cf. Rhetorius, *Astrological Compendium*, Chapter 26.

[2] This is because the *dominant* sign would rise before the other one and be in the MC when the other one came to the ASC.

[3] That is, is *dexter* to the other star. And this is because it moves to the nearest angle before the other star.

[4] The Greek word means 'neighborhood' or 'juxtaposition'.

they are related to each other by aspect [and are both] in the terms of the same star.

23. *Void of Course.*

It is termed *void of course* whenever the Moon does not conjoin any one [of the planets] either *zodiacally* or *partilely* or by *aspect* or by *kollêsis* or within 30 degrees of the next conjunction or when it is going to make a conjunction [with the Sun].[1] And nativities of this sort [are] undistinguished and lacking in advancement.

24. *Casting Rays.*[2]

The *preceding* star[3] *casts a ray* to the *following* one by aspect; for example, the one in Aries casts a square aspect to the one in Capricorn and a trine aspect to the one is Sagittarius; and the one following *beholds* the preceding one, and, when the preceding one is moved over it, it *prevails* over the following one, as was said previously, but it does not *cast a ray* [to it].[4] For the *sight* of every beam is borne to the *front*, and the *ray* itself to the *rear*; and then it is necessary to see whether it *casts its ray* only zodiacally or whether it applies partilely.[5]

---

[1]Note that this definition differs from the modern one, in which the Moon is said to be 'void of course' if it does not make another aspect before it leaves the sign that it is in.

[2]Cf. Hephaestio, *Apotelesmatics*, i. 16, and Rhetorius, *Astrological Compendium*, Chapter 21.

[3]This means "*preceding* counter-clockwise in the direction of the zodiac," i.e. on the left of another Planet, which is said to "follow" behind it.

[4]So, a Planet *casts a ray* to a Planet on its *right*, which *ray* is *beheld* by that Planet. Rather as if one person shone a flashlight forward on another person, and that person looked back and beheld the person shining the light.

[5]That is, whether the planet is merely in a sign that is in aspect to the sign the other Planet is in, or whether the two Planets are actually in partile aspect.

And there are categories about these two, for having put the *casting a ray* star by square from the 'meeting' sign to the 'one of the following [star]', for example the one in Cancer *casting a ray* to one in Aries, and the one in Aries *beholding* the one in Cancer. And if it is a malefic, they say it is *anaeretic.*[1] For the one *casting a ray* is *anaeretic*, not the one that is *beholding*. But the one that is in opposition both *casts a ray* and *beholds*. Of course the one never *casts a ray* by trine, for it supports itself on the *ray* towards the square that is quite near, rather than on the trine, just as it is easier in the case of the trine to assume its sympathy. That is the way then that these things are.

And Thrasyllus says that *casting a ray* is a destruction, and those are *anaeretic* that are occupying a position in the square configurations or in the oppositions in the interval between the ASC degree and the testimony of the trines that are not incurring destruction. And the one they carry from anywhere, it will not carry the ray across, he says, whether from the right or from the left into the succedent of the ASC or of the star holding the rulership of the Moon, then it will be the *aphetic* place. And he says that if the Moon chances to be having the Ruler of the Nativity with her or by opposition, we shall make the *aphetic* place to be from the Ruler of the Nativity; for example, if the Moon was in Sagittarius with Jupiter, or if Jupiter is in Gemini with the Moon herself being in Sagittarius, we shall begin from Jupiter.

25. *Chariots.*

Stars are said to be *in their own chariots* whenever they are posited in their own domicile or triplicity or exaltation

---

[1]That is, it indicates death or destruction. Cf. Ptolemy, *Tetrabiblos*, iii. 10.

and [are also] in their own terms. And a star will also be most powerful thus, even if it has come under the Sunbeams, for [then] it is even more powerful. And if it also has an oriental [position], or if it chances to be angular and it aspects the Moon, it will make nativities possessing power and ruling.

26. *Joint Possession.*

Joint possession is whenever the one jointly possessing the sign is present in or aspects its own domicile; and the one that is jointly ruling is in *joint possession* of the sign; and it is jointly ruling when [the sign] is its domicile or its exaltation.[1]

27. *Incongruity of Position.*

Incongruity of position is said whenever the diurnal [stars] occupy the domiciles or the exaltations of the nocturnal [stars], or when the nocturnal [stars] occupy those of the diurnal [stars], or whenever the stars posited in the signs are effective, and the rulers of the signs are afflicted, since they happen then to be ineffective.

28. *Affliction.*

It is said to be an *affliction* whenever a [star] is aspected by the malefics, or when it is *besieged*, or is in application with a malefic, or is coming into a *kollêsis* [with it], or is being opposed, or prevailed over, or when its house-ruler is a malefic badly situated and cadent in ineffective [houses].

---

[1]This definition is awkward. The term is more clearly defined by Rhetorius, *Compendium of Astrology*, Chapter 30 "*Joint possession* is when two planets are in a single sign or behold it—it happening to be the domicile of one and the exaltation of the other."

29. Doryphory.

There are three kinds of *doryphory*.[1] First, if there is an angular [star] in its own domicile or exaltation, [and] another [star] posited in its own domicile or exaltation beholds it by aspect, casting its ray upon the preceding degree of that one. For example if the Sun is in Leo [and] Saturn opposes it from Aquarius, or Jupiter trines it from Sagittarius; or again, if Jupiter is posited in Cancer and Mars in Capricorn opposes [it], or if it is in Sagittarius and Mars trines [it] from Aries, or Mercury opposes [it] from Gemini; or if the Moon is posited in Cancer and Mars trines [it] from Scorpio, or Jupiter or Venus from Pisces; or again, if the Moon is posited in Taurus [and] Venus or Jupiter sextile [it] from Pisces; or if the Moon [is] posited in Cancer [and] Venus sextiles it from Taurus or Jupiter or Venus trines [it] from Pisces. And this is a great nativity if the rulers of the sect are in *doryphory*, and not a bad one otherwise, except if the malefics do not chance to be there, and these harm those and help those. For a star acting in its own domicile or exaltation is effective.[2]

We call another kind of *doryphory* that of "the casting of rays." For example, if a Light is angular in the ASC and posited in the domicile of another [star] [and] a star of its sect casts a ray, to the Sun in its preceding degree or to the Moon in its following [degree], throwing the ray towards that one

---

[1]The word *doryphory* literally means 'spear-bearer', and it was used commonly to designate an armed guard who was the guardian of the king. In astrology it means a planet closely associated with the Sun or the Moon. Cf. this lengthy chatper with Ptolemy, Tetrabiblos, iii. 4 and iv. 3; Hephaestio, *Apotelesmatics*, i. 17; and Rhetorius, *Astrological Compendium*, Chapter 23. Ptolemy mainly speaks of Planets that are close to the Sun or Moon, such as "morning stars" or "evening stars," which is similar to Porphyry's third kind of *doryphory*, and this was probably the original definition. But Hephaestio and Rhetorius give definitions that are merely copied versions of Porphyry's three kinds of *doryphory*.

[2]The text has *anenergetos* 'ineffective', but we should read simply *energetos* 'effective'.

which moves according to an equal-sided line. And all the *doryphories* by trine are stronger than those by square or opposition or sextile.

There is [also] a third kind of *doryphory*. If [there is] a star posited in the ASC or in the MC by day in a diurnal nativity or by night in a nocturnal one, the [stars] that precede or follow it will be its *doryphories* according to the following scheme. The Sun will be *doryphoried* by those [stars] that precede [it], and the Moon by those that follow it within 7 degrees; however, those [stars] that are *doryphories* that precede it by 15 degrees do not harm the Sun if they are oriental and have force. And according to these same [conditions], the Sun itself can be a *doryphory* to an angular [star] of its own sect, and the Moon similarly. The *doryphories* become out-of-sect whenever the diurnal [stars] are *doryphories* to the nocturnal ones, or the nocturnal ones to the diurnal ones; but nevertheless, if the *doryphory* is made by benefics, not even in this case will the nativity be undistinguished.

30. *The Ruler of the Nativity and the Lord and the Ruling [Star]*.

Furthermore, it is necessary to explain in detail in what [respect] the *Ruler of the Nativity*,[1] and the *Lord*, and the *Ruling [star]* differ from each other. For the ancients devising the nomenclature did not distinguish their function. For each has its own force, just as the sailor and the steersman. We shall explain, therefore, in what respect they differ from each other.

---

[1] This is the *oikodespotês* literally, the 'house-ruler', by which is meant the ruler of a sign of the zodiac. But it is often used in astrology to mean "Ruler of the Nativity," and that is what Porphyry is attempting to make clear.

Some, then, put the Sun to rule by day and the Moon to rule by night; and this will be accurately set forth thus: in a diurnal nativity, the Sun, if it is rising in the east, will take the ruling position; but when the Sun is declining in the west, if the Moon happens to be in the east, she will take [that position], and if she is succedent to the ASC,[1] through her rising into the east; but if they are both cadent in the west, the ASC will have the ruling position. And in a nocturnal nativity, if the Moon rises into the east, she will take the ruling position, but if she is declining into the west and the Sun is under the earth succedent to the ASC, he will be in the ruling position.

And if both of them happen to be under the earth, angular or succedent, the Moon will have the ruling position because of the sect,[2] but if she is found to be cadent, and the [Sun] is angular, he [will be selected]. For the angular one of the Lights and the one that is more in the east and of the sect is judged to be the Ruling [Star]. And if both of them are cadent, the ASC will obtain the ruling position then. And whenever you appoint the Ruling [Star][3] from this, the House-ruler and the Joint House-ruler will be left remaining. For the Lord of the sign in which the Ruling [Star] is will be the House-ruler, and it is necessary to look at it and the Joint House-ruler of the terms to see how they move and in what aspect they are, and whether they behold the ASC or the Moon, for the whole distinction will be from these. And

---

[1] That is, in the 2nd house.

[2] The Moon is the ruler of the nocturnal sect.

[3] A scholium of Demophilus: "as soon as you appoint the Ruling [Star], look at the *anaeretic* rays of the malefics, the squares, the oppositions, [and] the sextiles, as far as the ninetieth degree, and from the rising times is generated the evident length of life. A benefic casting a ray into the [parts] following the *anaeretic* degree as far as the 5th degree or even more, if it is the same term, is able to counteract the evil."

some simply put the Lord of the Terms of the ASC as the Ruler of the Nativity and the Joint-ruler of the sign.

The Lord of the Nativity on the one hand and the Ruler of the MC they define, particularly if it is angular [and] effective, but if not, the one that is close to the MC, for instance in the highest part of the nativity—which is the one ruling actions—and if not that one, then the one that is cadent to the MC. And the first, the Lord of the ASC or the one that is posited on it in the domicile and the terms, either the one of the Moon, or the one of the MC, or the one of the [Lot of] Fortune, or the one 7 days before birth, or within 7 days making a phase of the rising or the setting or of a station.[1] For this one of the cosmic sign is then being rendered authoritative by common consent and [chosen] to rule those being born, and if there are two of them, they put the one rising as being more powerful. To these they join the ruler of the preceding lunar conjunction[2]; and I say the Ruler of the Terms in which the conjunction of the Sun with the Moon occurred, if indeed the Moon is moving away from the conjunction; but if she is waning, the one becoming the Ruler of the Terms of the full Moon.

And from all these, the one posited [so that it is] harmonizing most with the nativity [is the] Ruler, i.e. the one posited in front, the most easterly, or the one that is most in its own domicile, and that has the most force for the scheme of the nativity and those that are mutually configured with it. And in connection with the Ruler that has been found, it is necessary to look at how [it is disposed], in those things that have been

---

[1]A scholium of Demophilus: It must signify that one must take not only the phase in the rising but also in the setting and in a station. But Dorotheus also says to include the setting phases of the revolving stars.
[2]That is, the new Moon.

said in order, and what is the power [derived] from this. For there is much dispute about this, and almost all of it is very difficult [to understand]. Sometimes, however, it happens that the same [star] is found to be both Ruler and House-ruler, whenever the Ruler that is found is the House-ruler of the dominant Light,[1] which same will preside over a great destiny.

31. *Obeying Signs.*

One sign *obeys* another sign, as Libra obeys Aries because Aries increases the [length of] the day, but Libra decreases it; [similarly] Pisces [obeys] Taurus because Taurus has more rising time and Pisces less; similarly Aquarius [obeys] Gemini, Capricorn Cancer, Sagittarius Leo, and Scorpio Virgo.[2]

32. *Equipollent Signs.*

Those signs are said to be *equipollent* to each other that have equal rising times and are parallel[3] to each other, as Aries and Pisces, and Virgo and Libra, and through the 3rd and 4th and 5th [pairs of] equal rising, as Taurus and Aquarius, Gemini and Capricorn, Cancer and Sagittarius, [and] Leo

[1] That is the ruler of the sign in which is placed the 'Light of the Time', i.e. the Sun if it is a diurnal nativity, or the Moon if it is a nocturnal one.

[2] These pairs of planets are based on the scheme of the early Alexandrian astrologers, which in effect puts the equinoxes and solstices at 15 degrees of the cardinal signs. The Hipparchean switch to the tropical zodiac, by moving the equinoxes and solstices to the 1st degree of the cardinal signs, invalidated the earlier arrangement. But it was firmly fixed in tradition, so Ptolemy cannily avoids giving any specific pairs of signs in *Tetrabiblos* i. 14, "Commanding and Obeying Signs," by saying that "they are disposed at an equal distance from the same equinoctial *sign*." (Robbins's translation, but italics mine.)

[3] The Greek text has *ephexês* 'in order', but I think 'parallel' is better—that is, one on one side of the 0-180 line and the other opposite it on the other side of the line.

and Scorpio. But some say these only *hear* each other, but do not *see* each other because of the shadow of the earth.[1]

33. *Seeing Signs and the Length of the Day.*

Seeing [signs] are those that deliver the lengths of the days and nights in equal hours. For since the greatest length of the day in the Fifth Clime, when the Sun is in Cancer, is 15 [equinoctial] hours and the least, when the Sun is in Capricorn, is 9 [equinoctial] hours, and the lengths are equal in Libra and Aries, there will be in Gemini and Leo a day of 14 [equinoctial] hours, in Taurus and Virgo [a day] of 13 hours, in Aries and Libra of 12 hours, in Scorpio and Pisces of 11, [and] in Aquarius and Sagittarius of 10 hours. These then are the signs that see each other.[2]

34. *Inconjunct Signs.*

Those [signs] are *inconjunct* each other that are related to each other neither by [equidistance from] the tropics nor by aspect.[3]

---

[1]These are properly called *commanding and obeying* signs. They are the pairs of signs that are equally distant from an *equinox*, but in opposite hemispheres; and they consequently have equal rising times. But the Alexandrian founders originally reckoned the pairs as being equidistant from an equinoctial *sign* (e.g. Taurus & Pisces, Gemini & Aquarius, etc.); those pairs were also cited by the authors mentioned in the next note.

[2]These are the original pairings of signs supposed to be on either side of the summer *solstice*. But the Alexandrian founders customarily reckoned by whole signs; hence, for them the entire *sign* of Cancer constituted the *solstice*. These same pairings of signs are given by Manilius, *Astronomica*, 2.485-519; Vettius Valens, *Anthology*, i. 7; Dorotheus, *Pentateuch*, cited by Hephaestio, *Apotelesmatics*, ii. 23; Paul of Alexandria, *Introduction*, Chapter 8; and Maximus. Rhetorius, *Astrological Compendium*, Chapter 19, gets them mixed up with the *commanding and obeying* signs. However, since the solstice is actually at the beginning of Cancer, the pairings should be Gemini and Cancer, Taurus and Leo, and Aries and Virgo. And Firmicus, *Mathesis*, ii. 29, gets it right.

[3]We must remember here that the ancients only recognized the sextile, the square,

35. *Cadent [and Succedent Houses].*

The 4 [houses] that precede the angles are called *cadent*, and similarly the 4 following the angles are called *succedent*. They say the *eastern* region of a nativity is the one from the ASC degree to the MC; the *southern*, the one is from the MC to the DSC; the *western*, the one from the DSC to the IMC; and the *northern*, the one from the IMC to the ASC.

36. *Effective Signs.*

According to Timaeus, 7 signs are *effective* in each nativity—the 4 angles, the 2 trines of the ASC, and for the remaining one, the cadent of the MC[1]. And the remainder are ineffective. But many times, if the majority of the degrees of the rising sign have already risen before it, and the last degrees are rising, the succedent sign will be *jointly effective* with the rising sign.[2]

37. *The Conception Sign of the Sun.*

They say that *the conception sign of the Sun* is [the one] in the tenth month, [namely] the [one that is the] sinister square of the one from which you set out; for when it was there, the conception occurred.[3] And on the seventh month the opposition.

---

the trine, and the opposition as aspects. Consequently pairs of signs like Aries & Taurus, or Aries & Virgo were not "in aspect"; hence, they were said to be *inconjunct*. And they are of course not equidistant from the tropics.

[1]Namely, the 9th house.

[2]Here, as often, the word 'sign' is used instead of 'house' because the Sign-House system of houses is assumed. In this, the original house system, the rising sign constitutes the first house, the next sign the second house, etc. But Porphyry is saying that if, say, the 28th or the 29th or the 30th degree of the rising sign is the ASC degree, then you should also consider the next sign to be as effective as the rising sign.

[3]By 10th month, of course, Porphyry means what we would call the 9th month.

38. *The Conception Sign of the Moon.*

As for the Moon, others take another [approach]. And Antiochus says two approaches are true. "Observe," he says, "how much of the Moon anyone is born in,[1] and to that number add 5, and take away 29 in return from the month in which the birth took place, and wherever the number leaves off, then was the day of conception. Be sure then to step back in the table in which sign the Moon was then."[2]

But Petosiris says, that "wherever the Moon was at the [time of] conception, that same [place] or its opposite will rise at birth. And wherever the Moon was posited at [the time of] birth, that same place was rising at the [time of] conception."

Furthermore, some also take the ASC of conception in the same way. Observe which particular degree of the sign is rising at the [time of] birth, and multiplying what has risen by the full [number of] hours and measuring off the product by 30 degree [intervals] from the rising sign at birth, and wherever the number falls, there [is the] rising [degree] [at the time of] the conception of the seed.[3]

The rule simply says to count back 9 months (or signs), and there is the Sun sign of conception, which is in sinister square to the Sun sign at birth.

[1] That is, on what day of the lunar month the person was born. Cf. Leopold of Austria, *Compilation of the Science of the Stars*, Treatise 7, "By whatever number of degrees the conjunction of the Sun and the Moon or the full Moon preceded the nativity, that same number of degrees will be the angle of a human nativity…"

[2] None of this makes any sense. The passage is obviously corrupt. Vettius Valens, *Anthology*, i. 21, gives elaborate rules for making conception calculations. But they depend upon the distance of the natal Moon from the DSC degree.

[3] Another cryptic set of rules.

39. *The Dodecatemory [of the Moon].*

The dodecatemory of the Moon is taken properly, first by looking at how many degrees of the sign the Moon has; of that [number] measure off by 2½ degrees to the succeeding [signs], and wherever the number leaves off, there is the *dodecatemory*. For example, let the Moon have 13 [degrees] of Aries; give to Aries 2½, to Taurus 2½, to Cancer 2½, to Leo 2½, then the *dodecatemory* is in Virgo, the domicile of Mercury. The *dodecatemory* of the Sun is taken similarly. [And the degree] of the ASC is taken in the same fashion. For whenever it is seen which degree is rising, measure off of that number by [multiples of] 2½ degrees.[1]

But some take the *dodecatemory* of the Moon otherwise. Seeing how many degrees of the Moon[2] it has, from all those,[3] take away how many thirties it has, and the remaining ones[4] distribute by 2½ from whichever sign the Moon holds. And if it does not have [more than] 30, take away from those it has by 2½, [and] distribute them.

And it is necessary to determine the ASC [degree], by calculating very accurately according to the table.

40. *Masculine and Feminine Signs.*

The [signs that are] *masculine* by sect are those of the Sun, Jupiter, and Saturn. And let [every other one of] the signs be

---

[1]Note that the final measurement is made from the beginning of the sign that the Moon or the Sun or the ASC is in.

[2]Reading *tês Selenês* 'of the Moon' rather than *toû Hliou* 'of the Sun'.

[3]This must mean the total longitude of the Moon (measured from 0° ♈) rather than its longitude measured from the beginning of its sign).

[4]Which would be its longitude from the beginning of its sign.

masculine [starting] from Aries. The [signs that are] *feminine* [by sect] [are those] of the Moon, Mars, and Venus. Let every other one of the [signs] be *feminine* [starting] from Taurus. But choose individually [from] the *feminine* [signs] Capricorn for Saturn, Pisces for Jupiter; and of the *masculine* [signs] Aries for Mars, [and] Libra for Venus; but [in the case] of Mercury, choose [both] Gemini and Virgo, for it has those in common.

41. *The Rising Time of the Signs.*

They reckon the zodiacal times in accordance with the *risings of the signs*. For every degree of each sign is powerful at a certain time. But all of these [rising times] did not harmonize with each other, but the ancients made the risings differently. For nearly all of them, in the clime of Alexandria and of those cities situated nearby, the said Aries rises in 21:40, and Taurus in 25:00, Gemini in 28:20, Cancer in 31:40, Leo in 35:00, Virgo in 38:20, Libra in 38:20, Scorpio in 35:00, Sagittarius in 31:40, Capricorn in 28:20, Aquarius in 25:00, Pisces in 21:40.[1] But, for the clime of Alexandria, Ptolemy makes Aries rise in 20:53, and Taurus in 24:12, Gemini in 29:55, Cancer in 34:37, Leo in 35:36, Virgo in 34:47, Libra in 34:47, Scorpio in 35:36, Sagittarius in 34:37, Capricorn in 29:55, Aquarius in 24:12, Pisces in 20:53.[2]

------

[1]These are the traditional rising times established by an arithmetical progression invented by the Babylonians and adopted by the Alexandrian astrologers in the second century B.C. They are of course only an approximation, as can be seen by comparison with Ptolemy's rising times, which are correct, although calculated for a slightly lower latitude and with a slightly erroneous value of the Obliquity of the Ecliptic.

[2]These are the rising times given for 'Lower Egypt' (30N22) in *Syntaxis*, ii. 9, and also in more detail in the *Handy Tables*, which is probably where Porphyry found them.

Much indeed is the controversy, as to whether someone, not knowing the change in these, but recognizing the rising times of the ancients, imagined [himself] to be able to distribute those same times by the methods of Ptolemy. [Those who do so] miss the mark altogether, for there are two things that are necessary for finding the length of life—both the distribution of the terms among the five planets, and the rising times of the signs. There has been disagreement between the ancients and the newer [writers]. For Apollinarius in his disposition of the terms also disagrees with Ptolemy,[1] and both of them disagree with Thrasyllus and Petosiris and the other older [writers].[2]

And with regard to the risings of the signs, there is disagreement among them, which the newer [writers] think they have examined thoroughly by geometrical methods. Equally of course the announcements from the risings for the findings of the times are made by the ancients according to the dispositions of the houses of the risings—thoroughly examined it seemed in the finding of the times, so that not only do they show how to announce years approximately or even months, but also days and hours, although measuring the years from the rising times according to them, and measuring the *anaeretic* and *aphetic* places[3] from the terms according to them, and [consequently] being deceived by those.

---

[1]That is, Apollinarius's system of terms differed from Ptolemy's own system of Terms as shown in the *Tetrabiblos*.

[2]That is, with the 'Terms According to the Egyptians'.

[3]The *aphetic place*, literally 'the starting place', is that point in a horoscope from which a direction or profection indicative of the lifespan of the native is measured. This original term has been replaced in more recent astrological literature by the term *hyleg* (from the Arabic *hîlâj* from the Middle Persian *hîlâk* 'letting loose', a translation of the Greek *aphetès* 'starter'). The *anaeretic place*, literally 'the destructive place', is the termination of a direction or profection that is assumed to indicate the death of the native.

Therefore, it is necessary that they not be mixed together, and that we do not make the mistake of changing from one [system] into the other [while using] Ptolemy's method "About the Times of Life"[1] with the methods agreeable to Ptolemy concerning the rising times, and the tracing back of the terms, [for] he was using them and those same for the terms. And it is necessary to make use of the others similarly when we declare those things as useful for the reading of those things. I had [previously] taken for myself those things said by the Chaldeans, and when we had examined the saying of Ptolemy, we tried also to prove those same by trial, whether they are in accordance with the opinion of Ptolemy.

Therefore, we shall relate [their method], so that [it will be understood] whenever one wants to try out with them the years from the rising times—[that is], to find by diligent re-search the life events of the natives. For it is from the ASC degree, and not from any other place that they are especially found, and from the rising times, and those of the life in each instance, to show with them [by reckoning] from the sign of the ASC. Then too of course they judged the major times of the whole life by taking the rising times of the signs. For it is not indeed [simply] according to the taking of the seasonal hours that is the only method of these, but also by taking the allotment accurately from the yearly times that are there. For having understood each sign of 30 degrees to be the ruler of 30 years, just as the 360 degrees of the circle has 360 years, therefore one degree is a single year. And we have used the times [of life] according to the rising times of the signs.

Therefore, with Aries rising under the clime of Alexandria in 21 degrees and 40 minutes—that is to say, that according

---

[1]This is a reference to *Tetrabiblos*, iii. 10 (Robbins's edition).

to its rising time [it is] 21 years and 8 months. And therefore distributing the 21 years and the 8 months by the 30 degrees of the sign, I found for each degree 8 months and 20 days. And since Taurus rises under that same clime in 25 times, i.e. in 25 years, the 25 years being divided by 30 degrees, gives 10 months to each degree of Taurus.[1]

If then we are agreeing with those [numbers], even though Ptolemy had also worked out the [numbers] of the rising times, by using them one readily takes the distributions of the major times to have been delivered into each degree of the signs. And since Ptolemy had declared the rising times to be made differently, indeed those others believed it is necessary to divide them according to analogy, which he worked out in the *Handy Tables*[2] of the rising times of the 30 degrees of each sign.

42. *In How Many Times Each Degree Rises by Signs.*

In how many times each degree rises is found thus[3]: for since the [number of] degrees of each sign is 30, the rising-times either exceed [that number] or are deficient. For the rising-times of Aries in the First Clime [are] 24°20′, of

---

[1]Again, these are the traditional rising times as mentioned above.

[2]The *Handy Tables* were a set of astronomical tables prepared by Ptolemy that summarized the tables in his larger work, the *Almagest* and provided some useful auxiliary tables. Most astrologers from the fourth century on used the *Handy Tables* because they were more convenient.

[3]Note that the procedure that follows (using Ptolemy's rising times) determines the *average* rising time of a degree in each of the 12 signs, not the rising time of a specific degree. Hence, it is only an approximation to the actual rising-time of a particular degree. For example, for the Clime of Meroê (16N27) the average rising-time of a degree of Aries is 0°48′40″, but the average rising-time of a degree of Taurus is 0°54′08″ (using the correct rising time for Taurus). This discrepancy gets larger with an increase in latitude. Obviously (to us, at least), the use of an average rising-time for a degree would inject some error into determining the time when a primary direction would act.

Taurus in the same clime 33°23′,[1] [etc.]. In order that we may know in how many [times] each degree rises, we will reduce the rising-times of the entire sign to sixtieths. For example, in Aries, reducing the 24°20′ to sixtieths, we will find the total [number of] minutes [to be] 1460. Dividing these by 30 (for that many degrees are in each sign), we will find each degree to have 48′40″.

By this same analogy, getting the times of the risings of each sign in years or months, we will apportion to each day the times allotted, both to the months, and also to the years. But we shall do so thus: the rising-times of Aries in the Clime of Meroê being 24°20′, we shall multiply by the 12 months. The 24 degrees become (counting [1] for each month of the year) 288; the 20 minutes (look what part it is of 60—it is 1/3), which [part] of a year having taken, makes 4 months; altogether [then] it becomes 292 months, and I divide by 30 degree intervals, and they make 9 months for each degree, and 22 months are left over, which changing into days, I have 660 days; these again I divide by 30, and it makes 22 days. So that applies to each degree of Aries and of Pisces—for in all [climes] they rise in equal times. Therefore, in the Clime of Meroê, for each degree there are 9 months [and] 22 days. Doubling these degrees [gives] 18 months [and] 42 days,[2] and the triple of them [is] 2 years 5 months [and] 6 days. This same approach [is used] both for each sign and for each clime.[3]

---

[1]As A. Rome notes in the apparatus to the Greek text, Ptolemy's rising time for Taurus in the clime of Meroê is only 27°04′, not 33°23′, which is close to the rising time for Cancer 33°26′. Whether the error is due to Porphyry himself or to one of the copyists is unknown. (Possibly, a line has dropped out of the Greek text, so that the translation should read ". . . of Taurus in the same Clime <27°04′, of Gemini in the same Clime 31°06′, and Cancer in the same Clime> 33°23′.")

[2]It should be 18 months and 44 days.

[3]Scholium. However that division has yielded the rising-times, both the month and also the rising-times, for the years are also observed from these. In all climes

43. *The Determination of the Angular, Cadent, and Succedent [Houses] for a Particular Degree.*

Ptolemy says in his [chapter] "The Length of Life"[1] that the [region] around the ascending twelfth[2] is certainly to be taken as *aphetic*, [i.e.] from 5 of those degrees rising before the horizon itself down to the remaining 25 degrees rising beneath. He took [those degrees] rising before the ASC and the 25 degrees following as constituting the 30 degrees of the twelfth.[3] But this is done in these climes when the equinoctial sign rises[4] because the semicircle of the commanding [signs]—those rising from Aries to Virgo—always makes the eastern quadrants greater than the whole 90 degrees, but the western [quadrants] less. Conversely, if one of the obeying [signs] rises, it makes the eastern quadrants less than, and the western [quadrants] more than, the 90 degrees.

And [he says] plainly[5] that the degrees of the quadrant, those from the MC to the ASC, must be divided into three [parts], and the third allotted to the ASC and 5 degrees of however much is taken as rising before, [and] to have the remainder following; and to do similarly also in the rest of the quadrants. But if anyone says, when alluding to the [particular] number of degrees for any house, [that] a sixth must be put before, he does not understand [the procedure] rightly, for if by chance there are 72 degrees between the MC and the

---

the rising-times are transformed [thus] for each sign and each degree.

[1] *Tetrabiblos* iii. 10 (Robbins's edition).

[2] By *twelfth* he means *house*.

[3] This is plainly a reference to the Equal House method of House division.

[4] This is an early attempt to try to adapt what Ptolemy says to a quadrantal method of House Division. It is of course futile.

[5] Not so! Ptolemy gives no such instructions for house division. He merely states that certain houses in the hemisphere above the earth are in aspect to the 1st house as he defined it. And his statement is consistent with a slightly modified version of what we call 'Equal House', in which each house has 30 degrees.

ASC, the following quadrant will obviously have 108 degrees; then, in the one case there will be 1/6 of 24 degrees, and in the other 1/6 of 36 degrees; and so the degrees before the MC will be 4 degrees [with] 20 degrees following, and in addition, from the 11th and the 12th [houses], 48 degrees, and left over for the ASC only 4 degrees. For there were altogether 72 degrees, from which [having subtracted 68 degrees, there are only] 4 degrees remaining which the ASC will have. [But] it is necessary by this method to have 6 [in the following quadrant], for 6 is 1/6 of 36.

Such a method, therefore, is ineffective; and not even in the rising times, for example, is it useful, therefore, to assign 30° to each house. For with the 6th degree of Pisces rising in the 5th or 6th clime down to the Midheaven under the earth,[1] the rising times are hardly 60, and thus we will not have anything to give to the third house; therefore, this cannot be done, and 30 degrees cannot be allotted to each house. For again, with Aquarius rising and Sagittarius culminating, 70 degrees are found in between, and 90 was required if indeed each will have 30 degrees; out of necessity, then, there remains the 5 degrees rising before the ASC angle, and the remaining amount still needed to go with that from the quadrantal distribution.[2]

44. *What Sort of Part of the Body Each Sign was Allotted.*

Moreover, each one of the signs was allotted some parts of the body, which it is necessary to be mindful of whenever they speak of injuries. Aries [rules] the head; Taurus, the ten-

---

[1] That is, the IMC.

[2] Here again Porphyry is comparing the Equal House Division of the houses, which is what Ptolemy had in mind, with what we call the Porphyry House Division. Naturally they do not agree, for only in the Equal House system (or in the older Sign-House system) can we have 30° in each house.

dons and the neck; Gemini, the shoulders and the arms; Cancer, the chest and the sides; Leo, the diaphragm and the stomach and the belly; Virgo, the abdomen and the flanks; Libra, the kidneys and the buttocks; Scorpio, the pudenda and the hidden parts and the generative parts; Sagittarius, the knees, and according to some, the groin and the hollows of the elbows; Capricorn, the loins and the hips; Aquarius, the calves and the ankles; Pisces, the feet.

45. *What Sort of Part [of the Body] Each Star Rules.*

In accordance with those things that are allotted to the stars, he says of those things that are internal, that Saturn [rules] the moister phlegmatic [parts] and the throat and loosening of the bowels; and Jupiter, the liver and the fatty tissue around it, and the sinews under the throat; and Mars, the blood and the kidneys and the spermatic passages; and Venus, the lungs and the bile; and Mercury, the hearing, the blood-vessels, and the tongue; and the Sun, the heart, and the respiration, that is the sensory movement, and the sense of sight—in a male on the right side, in a female on the left. And the Moon, in general, [rules] the whole body, but particularly her own [parts]—the spleen, the membranes, and the marrow, and the sight of a male on the left, but of a woman on the right.

And of the things outside [the body], Saturn rules chronic complaints, moist and chilling, and also old and stored up things, foundations and lands, old things and elder persons, and sterile and childless persons, sailors, [instances] of complete and deep and concealed wickedness, and false accusation, and slander, envy, and misery, and the most terrible [things], and prisons, and letting the hair grow long, and shamelessness, and everything most abominable, and severe tortures. Acting in its own places and chariots, and well configured in the nativity, it does help by supplying improvements from damage to others; but badly configured, it causes hardships and misfortunes. And it is called *Phainon*.[1]

And the [star] of Jupiter [rules] magnificence or glory, dignity, enjoyment, and also fatness, and also rulership and distinction, and many children, and approbation by the leadership and the common people. And it is called *Phaethon*.[2]

And the [star] of Mars is fiery and bloody and like a branding iron. Therefore it speaks of the hot blood in us, as was said, and of the spermatic impulse and of feminine fetuses, of action and of both dangers, and courage, and anger, and daring, and violence, and perilous affairs, and of severe suffering, of military service, and both of war and the employment of iron, and wounds, and all of those things that happen with quickness and panic. And it is called *Pyroeis*.[3]

And the Sun governs breath and the perceptive spirit that is in us, and the motion of breathing, and the paternal or the principal person.

And the [star] of Venus, being near to the Sun, and having greatness and shining by its brilliance, †when the smoke, just as it does with a fire burning above the lying below of that flat, it shines†,[4] it is seen best shaped and bright. Then, through the great cheerfulness of its light, it rules shapeliness, beauty, cleanliness, brilliance of life, neatness, being crowned, priesthood, wearing gold, very delicate [things or

---

[1] Greek for "shining."

[2] Greek, another word for "shining."

[3] Greek for "fiery."

[4] The Greek text is corrupt. Perhaps it should read, 'just like a fire burning above the ground shines through the smoke'.

conditions]. And through its presence and its casting beams of sympathy through the living element of the cosmos, it rules tender love, desire, longing, marriage, religion, skill in the arts of the Muses, and well-arranged beginnings, and the theatre. It is called *Phosphoros*.[1]

And the [star] of Mercury, being joined to the Sun, appears to be alternating,[2] and is more rarely seen.[3] And always when it has been disposed very near the forward beam of the Sun, and very often when it is rising and setting under the Sun beams, it indeed rules those things that are very near to the authoritative part of the soul, to the ruling element of the mental motion, of wisdom and reason and knowledge, and those things directed by reason—education, commerce, occupation, friendship, fellowship, agreement, companionship, and assistance. And it also [indicates] younger persons, children too, and nurslings. And it is called *Stilbon*.[4]

And the Moon, the one that is nearest to the Earth, and the one having separations from all [the other stars],[5] and attending upon the magnitude of it lying close to the Earth; it rules all our body and its health, and the condition, and the mother, and women in authority.

---

[1]Greek for 'light-bearing'.

[2]The Greek word *palmôdès* ordinarily means 'throbbing', 'pulsating', 'quivering'; in Modern Greek 'vibrating' or 'shaking'. If this is what Porphyry wrote, its meaning was perhaps 'alternating', referring to Mercury's moving back and forth fairly often from one side of the Sun to the other side.

[3]Mercury is more difficult to observe because it is close to the Sun and is always seen not far above the horizon.

[4]Greek. Still another word for 'shining'.

[5]Since the Moon moves the fastest, it can both apply to and separate from all the other stars (Planets).

46. *The Apparel and Dye or Complexions the [Stars] Rule.*

Saturn rules beaver-colored[1] dyeing; Jupiter, pale blue[2] and inclining a bit towards white; Mars, fiery—really flame-colored; the Sun, golden yellow; Venus, white-colored; Mercury, dark blue; the Moon, pale green.[3]

47. *The 36 Decans and their Paranatellonta and Faces.*

Although the zodiacal circle was divided into 12 divisions, i.e. into 12 *signs*, the ancients recommended another 36 divisions, which they called *decans*, and these they apportioned by sign to govern 10 degrees; therefore, they are called *decans*.[4] And the previously mentioned *paranatellonta*[5] lie under these decans in the zodiacal circle, and they have the *faces* of the 7 stars, which have sympathy with the stars that lie upon them.

For example, suppose the Sun to be in 10 degrees of Aries in the first *decan*, the *face* of Mars; then, since we have said that the Sun signifies the *spirit*, you will find the spirit of that [person] to be manly, irascible, fond of fighting, fond of weapons, and such like. Again, suppose the Sun to be in the

---

[1]Whatever color beavers were in antiquity—probably black or very dark brown, nearly black.

[2]The Greek text has *galaïzousês*, an otherwise unattested word that would appear to mean 'being milky white'. But I assume this is a blunder for *glaukizousês* 'being bluish-grey', since Zeus is the sky-god.

[3]This seems to be an unusual color assignment for the Moon.

[4]The Latin word *decanus* means 'someone presiding over ten persons'; hence, by analogy someone presiding over 10 degrees. The Egyptians gave each *decan* a name and considered the 36 *decans* to be minor divinities.

[5]This Greek word means 'rising alongside' and is said of the fixed stars that rise with specific degrees of the Zodiac in a particular geographic latitude. The word was popularized by Cyril Fagan (1896-1970) and has come to be recognized as a technical term in modern astrology.

20th degree of Aries, in the second *decan*, the *face* of the Sun; it signifies that [person] to be bright-spirited and ambitious and proud and not at all fond of fighting. Again, suppose the Sun to be in the 30th degree of Aries, in the third *decan*, the *face* of Venus; it signifies that [person] to be womanly-spirited, feminine in appearance, shameful, lustful, and such like. See how in a single sign they indicated three differences of spirit.[1]

And the astrological influences of the *decans* and their *paranatellonta* and the *faces* are included [in the works] by Teucer the Babylonian.[2]

48. *The Powers of the Bright Fixed Stars and their Parantellonta.*

The character of the signs and of the *paranatellonta* from the combination of the stars he has put below.[3] Therefore, they have in them bright stars and dim ones and the more gloomy ones. Observing these, the ancients said that the brightest of them were of the first magnitude, and the dimmer ones of the second magnitude, and the more gloomy ones of the third magnitude, and so on in sequence they found them down to the sixth magnitude. And they shared in common the natures of the planets, as we have said before, both those of

---

[1]This chapter agrees almost verbatim with the opening section of Rhetorius, *Astrological Compendium*, Chapter 10. Most likely both Porphyry and Rhetorius took it from Antiochus. The degrees mentioned are those at the end of each decan.

[2]See my translation of Rhetorius, *Astrological Compendium* (Tempe, Az.: A.F.A., Inc., 2009), which has the Significations of the Planets by Teucer as an appendix.

[3]This seems to imply that he (Porphyry) had included a table of the *paranatellonta* in his text. But if so, it was not copied by subsequent scribes and has not come down to us.

them that are located in the zodiacal circle, and those that are north of the zodiac, and those that are south of it. Taking note then of the brighter of those stars, they found that there were 30 of the first and second magnitude. Then, whenever these were found partilely in the ASC or in the MC, or configured with the Sun or the Moon, or with some star, they alter the nativity in accordance with their stated nature. For example, if it is of a benefic nature, the [native's] fortunes will be better, but if it is of a malefic nature, they will be worse.[1]

49. The Terms According to the Egyptians and Ptolemy, and the Bright and Dark Degrees.

Again, the ancients, cutting each sign into regions[2] or places that they called *terms*—not according to equal degrees, as we have said in the case of the decans—but divergently in accordance with another scheme, which they placed under the periods of the full periods of the stars; and I mean those which you will find earlier in them. But these degrees of the *terms* are constituted by sign. Some of them are found to be [the *terms*] of Jupiter, and others of Venus, and others of Saturn, and others of the rest of the planets.

Now whenever one of the stars is found in the domicile of a benefic and in the *terms* of a benefic having significance for the nativity, it makes the luck good. But if it is found in the domicile of a benefic, but in the *terms* of a malefic, the goodness of [the native's] luck is lessened. And if it chances to be in the domicile of a malefic and in the *terms* of a malefic, they

---

[1]This Chapter also agrees almost verbatim with Rhetorius, *Astrological Compendium*, Chapter 11.

[2]The Greek text has *emeiseis chôras* 'half regions', which makes no sense. I have omitted the word 'half'.

render his luck bad and obscure. Consequently the force of the *terms* alters the astrological signification of the stars, as was also said in the case of the faces of the decans.

Now Ptolemy in some *terms* does not agree with the Egyptians. Therefore I have been obliged to make mention of them and to set forth the *terms* in their own individual significations. And also the bright and the dark and dim degrees have no small force, if in fact the stars chance to have been found in the bright degrees. Wherefore, I was also obliged to list these previously.[1]

50. *The Melothesia of the Signs.*

He[2] arranged the *melothesia*[3] of man—which parts each of the signs rules and each of the stars—to make known to us the injuries and the illnesses that are happening to men from the Lots of Fortune and of the Daemon and of Injury and their rulers. For from those there are known, for the most part, the illnesses and the injuries. Now, having said all the preceding, following also the explanation of them which we have put plainly, I shall also[4] put next the manifest force of the configurations.[5]

---

[1]Unfortunately, the epitomator either did not find the tables in his exemplar or else he neglected to copy them, for they are absent from the received text of Porphyry's *Introduction* and also from Rhetorius's *Astrological Compendium*.

[2]This "He arranged" refers to Porphyry and was written by the epitomator who copied the excerpts of Porphyry's work that have come down to us (see the Translator's Preface above, p. vi).

[3]The word *melothesia* refers to a distribution of the parts of the body to the signs or to the planets. Here, it is to the signs.

[4]Reading *kai* 'also' with MS L rather than *kata* 'according to' with the other MSS and the CCAG editors.

[5]This chapter is nearly identical to Rhetorius, *Astrological Compendium*, Chapter 14.

51. *Trines, Squares, Sextiles, Oppositions, and Disjuncts Having Testimony to Each Other as in the System of Oppositions.*[1]

Differences of the trine and square and sextile configurations were established. And the *first* and greatest of all is the degree taken according to the *Handy Tables* of Ptolemy, as we have said in the previous [chapters]. And the *second* is the temporal, which Antigonus[2] and Phnaes the Egyptian[3] and some others established and named the equilateral triangle, with the risings of the signs. And the *third* is the zodiacal or common and general, into which we all wander.

For many times with the Sun in Leo around the 1st degree, and with Jupiter being in Sagittarius around the 5th degree, there appeared to be a trine of Jupiter to the Sun, but they were inactively configured with each other. For neither were they posited *platically* within the 120 degrees, nor were they placed *temporally* within the 120 degrees of the [horary] times, nor within the 120 degrees of *rising times*. {The rest then comes from the chapters about the planets.}[4]

Now the triangular side[5] is always called "zodiacal," which again had force, since both the degree-wise and the

---

[1]This chapter is very nearly identical to Rhetorius, *Compendium*, Chapter 15.

[2]Antigonus of Nicea, who wrote sometime after the death of the emperor Hadrian in 138 A.D. and before Porphyry wrote the present book in about 295 A.D. Antigonus's book contained Hadrian's horoscope and those of two other members of his family. They are cited by Hephaestio of Thebes (fl. c. 415) in his *Apotelesmatics* ii. 18, and are discussed in Neugebauer's & Van Hoesen's *Greek Horoscopes*.

[3]Nothing is known of Phnaes except that he must have written before Porphyry. Franz Cumont thinks that he may have been one of the sources of Antiochus of Athens. If so, then he wrote in the second century A.D. or earlier.

[4]Evidently a marginal note that was accidentally incorporated into the text.

[5]The classical astrologers viewed the aspects as being the *sides* of triangles, squares, or hexagons inscribed within the zodiacal circle. Hence I sometimes translate the Greek word *trigon* as 'trine' and sometimes as 'triangle'.

time-wise embraced it. Therefore, since we have established the side of the trines and squares and sextiles by degree in what follows through the tables of Ptolemy, now we have indicated the zodiacal, having believed it necessary to add also the *temporal* by an example.

Suppose the Sun to be in Aries in the 1st degree in the clime of Alexandria, and Jupiter in Leo in the 2nd degree, and Mars in Leo in the 5th degree. I do thus: the rising of Aries [is] 21°40′ [horary] times, and the rising of Taurus 25°00′ times, and the rising of Gemini 28°20′, and the rising of Cancer 31°40′; the times of the four signs make 106°40′; they are less than 120°00′ by 13°20′, which I will find around 11½ degrees of Leo.[1] For doubling the 35 times, they make 70 times; doing 11½ times these, I will find 805 times, these I divide by 60; they make 13°25' times. I combine the 106°40′; altogether they make 120°05′ times. And so the 11½ degree of Leo in the clime of Alexandria is found to be [the side of] an equilateral triangle prognosticating for the first degree of Aries. And we say that Jupiter is beheld by the Sun both *zodiacally* and *temporally*.

Since there remains 21°35′ times of Leo,[2] I add these to the second equilateral triangle thus: of Leo 21°35′, of Virgo 38°20′ times, of Libra 38°20′ times; altogether they make 98°15′ times; there remains again of the 120 times 21°45′.

---

[1]The rising times of the signs that he has given here are again the traditional rising times, not the Ptolemaic rising times. What Porphyry is doing here is finding where 120° of rising times (starting from the beginning of Aries) will be in Leo. Adding the rising times of Aries, Taurus, Gemini, and Cancer, he comes up 13°20′ short of 120°. So he then divides 13°20′ by 35 (which is the rising time of Leo) and multiplies the result by 30°. That gives him 11°26′ or 11½ as he calls it. And so he says that 120 rising times from the beginning of Aries comes to 11½ Leo.

[2]This is 35°00′ − 13°20′ = 21°40′ or approximately the 21°35′ that he mentions.

These I find around the 18 1/2 1/7 of Scorpio. for doubling the rising time of Scorpio, i.e. the 35 times, they become 70 times; multiplying these by 18 1/2 1/7, I find 1305 times, which I divide by 60; they become 21°45', which same I add to the 98°15'; altogether they make 120 times. And so the 18 1/2 1/7 degree[1] of Scorpio in the clime of Alexandria is found to be the second equilateral triangle prognosticating for the 11½ degree of Leo.

Again, since there remains 13°15' times of Scorpio,[2] I add to these the third equilateral triangle: of Scorpio 13°15', of Sagittarius 31°40', of Capricorn 28°20', of Aquarius 25, of Pisces 21°40'; altogether they make 119°55' times, which same prognosticate the third equilateral triangle of the zodiacal circle.[3] For the remaining 5 degrees were assigned to the 120 times in the first triangle. And by the same method you will also find the sextile and square aspects, which are called *temporal*.

52. The Times of the Angles, the Succedents, and the Cadents.

The ASC shows the *first age* [of life], the MC *middle age*, the DSC the *end* [of life], and the under earth angle (IC) *death* and the praise or disparagimg things happening after it.[4] And again, the cadent of the ASC signifies the labor pains

---

[1] 18 1/2 1/7 degrees = 18°38'. He got that by dividing 21°45' by 35°00' and multiplying the result by 30°.

[2] This is 35°00' − 21°45' = 13°15'.

[3] And here he has shown that his 18°38' Scorpio is close to 120° from the beginning of Aries. We may note that 18°38' Scorpio is approximately the contra-antiscion of 11°26' Leo, since both longitudes were arrived at by measuring 120 rising times both clockwise and counter-clockwise from the beginning of Aries.

[4] Here, the ages of man are reckoned in a clockwise direction like the motion of

of the parturient woman and the things happening in the womb when the native was in the belly; and the ASC the delivery and the times immediately after it; and the succedent to the ASC the end times of the first age. And the cadent of the MC signifies the first times of middle age; and the MC the middle times of middle age; and the succedent the end times. And the cadent of the DSC signifies the first times of the end time; and the DSC itself the middle times; and the succedent the end times. And the cadent of the IC signifies the time before death; and the IC itself death; and its succedent the time after death.

And each of these 12 houses has the 5 degrees rising before and the 25 degrees following after, if the quadrants happen to be 90 degrees, but if they are different numbers, divide the number of degrees in the quadrant into three equal thirds, and you will know how many degrees of the zodiac each house has.[1] For example, if the [arc of] the MC from the ASC has 96 degrees, the DSC has 84 degrees from the MC, and the under earth angle from the DSC 96 degrees, and the ASC from the under earth angle 84 degrees. Of these [degrees], distribute equally to each house the degrees that are its due from its own quadrant, making the beginning of the extent from the ASC degree and the 5 degrees rising before it; [by doing this], you will learn how the houses have [their division].

---

the Sun through the day and the following night. But in what follows, the subdivisions of each age are reckoned in the reverse order, apparently on the analogy that the sign that is the cadent comes to the angle before the sign that is the succedent.

[1]Here Porphyry explains how to calculate the cusps of what is now called the 'Porphyry System' of house division. This was the first of the quadrantal systems of house division. It had already been explained a century earlier by Vettius Valens in *Anthology* iii. 2, where he attributed its invention to an otherwise unknown astrologer named Orion. And he mentions the 5 degrees before the cusp that Ptolemy stated.

53. *In How Many Ways the Influences*
of the Planets are Generated.[1]

The astrological significations of the planets are made in *eleven* different ways. And the *first* of these is whenever the planet stands in a good house from the ASC or in one of the angles, or in the houses following the angles that the ASC aspects.

And the *second* is whenever the planet is in some place of its own worth, i.e. in its domicile, or its triplicity, or its exaltation, or its terms, or its face, or in the house in which it rejoices.

And the *third* is whenever the planet is not *retrograde*, but is *direct*.

And the *fourth* is whenever the planet is not joined to another malefic planet or in opposition or square to it.

The *fifth*, is whenever it is not applying to a planet, [that is] not aspecting the ASC, or to one that is in its fall.[2]

The *sixth*, is whenever it is being received.

The *seventh*, is whenever the superior planets, the masculine ones, i.e. Saturn, Jupiter, and Mars, are oriental or appearing in the east in the morning; and the inferior planets,

---

[1]This chapter is very similar to the Chapter "The Strength of the Planets" in Sahl ibn Bishr's *The Introduction to the Science of the Judgments of the Stars*, trans. by James Herschel Holden (Tempe, Az.: A.F.A., Inc., 2008), Book I (*Liber Introductorius*). It and the following chapters may have been translated from Arabic into Greek and mistakenly added to Porphyry's *Introduction*, by Demophilus.

[2]Some words seem to be missing. The Greek version of Sahl (edited in part in CCAG V. 3, p. 109) has, '5. That it is not configured with a star that is *cadent*, or with a star that is in its *fall*, or that the Moon is not in its *fall*.' And the Latin version has, 'The *fifth* is when it is not joined to a star that is *cadent* from the ASC, or to a planet that is in its own *fall*, or when it itself is not in its own *fall*.'

i.e. Venus, Mercury, and the Moon, are occidental, or appearing in the west in the evening.

The *eighth*, is whenever the planets are appearing in their own light, i.e. when the masculine planets are in the upper hemisphere by day, and in the lower hemisphere by night; but the feminine planets are by night in the lower hemisphere and by day in the upper hemisphere.

The *ninth*, is whenever the planets are in a fixed sign.

The *tenth*, is whenever the planets are in the Heart of the Sun, or [their] degree is next to its degree; for then the benefics strengthen their good and the malefics their evil.

The *eleventh*, is whenever the masculine planets are in masculine quadrants, and the feminine planets in feminine quadrants; and again, when the masculine planets are in masculine signs, and the feminine planets are in feminine signs.

54. *Exposition of the Testimony of the Planets.*[1]

This is the *testimony* of the planets, so that it is not ambiguous in the *yes* or *no*. Whenever a planet is in a [place] in which it has dignity, i.e. when it is in its own domicile, or in its triplicity, or in its exaltation, or in its terms, or in its face, then, if it signifies something, it fulfills it.

The astrological influences of the *Joys* of the planets are four [in number], and they are these: the *First Joy* is whenever Mercury falls in the ASC, or the Moon in the third

---

[1]The material in this Chapter is similar to that which is contained in the two Chapters "Testimony" and "The Joys of the Planets" in Sahl ibn Bishr's Book I.

house, Venus in the fifth, Mars in the sixth, the Sun in the ninth, Jupiter in the eleventh, and Saturn in the twelfth.

The *Second Joy*, is whenever Saturn is in Aquarius, Jupiter is in Sagittarius, Mars is in Scorpio, the Sun is in Leo, Venus is in Taurus, Mercury is in Virgo, and the Moon is in Cancer.

The *Third Joy*, is when the masculine planets *rejoice*, [i.e.] whenever they are oriental; and the feminine ones *rejoice*, whenever they are occidental.

The *Fourth Joy*, is whenever the masculine planets are in masculine quadrants and the feminine planets in feminine quadrants. Mercury *rejoices* with both, i.e. whenever it is with masculine [planets], it *rejoices* with them; and, whenever it is with feminine [planets], it *rejoices* with the feminine [planets].

55. *The Rays (Orbs) of the Planets.*[1]

The *rays* of the Sun reach as far as 30 degrees, 15 forward, and 15 backward. Those of the Moon, 24 degrees, 12 forward, and 12 backward; Saturn and Jupiter, 18 degrees, 9 forward, and 9 backward; Mars, 16, 8 forward, and 8 backward; Venus and Mercury, 14, 7 forward, and 7 backward.

---

[1]This chapter has the same orb numbers as the chapter *Scientia luminum vel orbium planetarum septem* 'Knowledge of the Lights or Orbs of the Seven Planets' in Sahl ibn Bishr's Book I.

Concordance of Similar Chapters in Antiochus's *Treasury*, Rhetorius's *Compendium*, and Porphyry's *Introduction*.[1]

Antiochus Treasury	Porphyry Introduction	Rhetorius Compendium	Porphyry Introduction
E3	3	1	45, 4
E1	4	2	
E5	7	3	
E6-9	8-11	4	44, 45
E12	15	5	7
E10	20	6	8
E11, 13-14	22-25	7	9
E16-17	26-29	8	10, 11
E28	30	9	11
E18-19	35	10	47
E18	36	11	48
E20-21	37-38	12	49
E22	39	13	(41)
E22	41	14	50
E4	44-45	15	51
	45	16	(34)
E10	47	17	
E11	48	18	
E12	49	19	(31, 33)
E14	50	20	37, 38
E15	51	21	38
E46	52	22	39, (41)
		23	
		24	
		25	
		26	
		27	
		28	
		36	(36)
		112	23

[1]The contents of these tables are derived from the two papers by David Pingree. The letter E before the chapter numbers in the left-hand column indicates the numbering of the chapters in the *Parisian Epitome*.

INDEX OF PERSONS

Petosiris, *astrologer*, viii.,28,31

Phnaes the Egyptian, *astrologer*, viii,44

Pingree, David, *scholar*, viii n.2&3,ix,xn.1,xv,51n.1

Pliny, *historian*, 6n.5,7n.3

Plotinus, *philosopher*, vii

Porphyry, *philosopher*, vii,viii,ix,x,xiin.3&4,1n.1,7n.2, 21n.1,22n.1,27n.2,30n.2,34n.1,39n.2,41n.1&3,43n.1&2,44 n.2&3,45n.1,47n.1,48n.1

Ptolemy, *science writer*, viii,1,7,19n.1,21n.1,25n.2,30,31, 32,33,34n.1,35,42-43,44-45,47n.1

Rhetorius the Egyptian, *astrologer*, viiin.3,ix,xi,xiii,xv,xvii, 17n.1,18n.2,20n.1,21n.1,26n.2,41n.1&2,42n.1,43n.1&5,44 n.1

Riske, Kris Brandt, *editor* xvii

Robbins, F. E., *translator*, 25n.2

Rome, A., *scholar*, 34n.1

Sahl ibn Bishr, *astrologer*, ix,xv,xvii,48n.1&2,49n.1,50n.1

Teucer of Babylon, *astrologer*, viii,41

Theon of Alexandria, *astronomer*, Bibliography

Thrasyllus, *astrologer*, 19,31

Timaeus, *astrologer*, viii

Weinstock, Stephen, *scholar*, x

Vettius Valens, *astrologer*, ix,26n.2,28n.2,47n.1

Wolf, Hieronomus, scholar, x

BIBLIOGRAPHY

Catalogus Codicum Astrologorum Graecorum (CCAG)
   [Catalogue of Greek Astrological Manuscripts]
   Brussels, 1898-1953. 12 vols. paper.

Dorotheus of Sidon
   Carmen Astrologicum.
   (The Pentateuch)
   ed. & trans. by David Pingree
   Leipzig: B. G. Teubner, 1976. xx,444 pp.

Firmicus Maternus, Julius
   Matheseos Libri VIII
   ed. by W, Kroll, F. Skutsch, & K. Ziegler
   Leipzig: B. G. Teubner, 1968. 2 vols.

Mathesis.
   ed. & trans. by James Herschel Holden
   Tempe, Az.: A.F.A., Inc., 2010.

Hephaestio of Thebes
   Apotelesmatica.
   ed. by David Pingree
   Leipzig: B. G. Teubner, 1973-1974. 2 vols.

Holden, James Herschel
   A History of Horoscopic Astrology.
   Tempe, Az.: A.F.A., Inc., 1996.
   Tempe, Az.: A.F.A., Inc., 2006. 2nd ed. rev.

Lilly, William
Christian Astrology...
London: John Partridge & Humphrey Blunden, 1647.
Exeter: Regulus Publishing Co., 1985. repr. in facs.

Neugebauer, O. and Van Hoesen, H. B.
Greek Horoscopes.
Philadelphia: The American Philosophical Society, 1959.

Neugebauer, Otto
A History of Ancient Mathematical Astronomy.
New York Heidelberg Berlin: Springer Verlag, 1975. 3 vols.

Parisian Epitome of Astrological Works.
edited in CCAG VIII 3.
Brussels: Henri Lamertin, 1912.

Paulus Alexandrinus
ΕΙΣΑΓΩΓΙΚΑ.
ed. by Emilia Boer
Leipzig: B. G. Teubner, 1958. XXVI,181 pp.

Paul of Alexandria
Introduction.
translated by James Herschel Holden
Tempe, Az.: A.F.A., Inc., 2010.

Pliny the Elder
Natural History.
trans. by various writers
Cambridge, Mass.: Harvard University Press
London: William Heinemann Ltd., 1949-1962. 10 vols.

Ptolemy, Claudius
  Tetrabiblos.
  ed. & trans. by F. E. Robbins, Ph.D.
  London: William Heinemann
  Cambridge, Mass.: Harvard University Press, 1940.

Ptolemy & Theon
  Procheiroi Kanones.
  [Ptolemy's & Theon's Handy Tables]
  ed. & trans. into French by the Abbé Nicolas Halma
  Paris: A. Bobée, 1823, 1825. 2 parts.

Rhetorius the Egyptian
  Astrological Compendium.
  trans. by James Herschel Holden
  Tempe, Az.: A.F.A., Inc., 2009. paper xx,222 pp. 22 cm.

Sahl ibn Bishr
  The Introduction to the Science
  of the Judgments of the Stars.
  trans. by James Herschel Holden
  Tempe, Az.: A.F.A., Inc., 2008. paper xxi,213 pp. 22 cm.

Vettius Valens
  Anthologiae.
  ed. by David Pingree
  Leipzig: B. G. Teubner, 1986. XXI, 583, [III}

SERAPIO OF ALEXANDRIA
ASTROLOGICAL DEFINITIONS

TRANSLATOR'S PREFACE

The Greek text of this short tract, entitled *Derived Names of the Configurations of the Stars*, was edited by Franz Cumont in CCAG 8.4 from the 15th century MS Parisinus graecus 2425. He notes that Serapio was apparently an early writer because his use of some words smacks of antiquity (e.g. *hôra* for ASC instead of *hôroskopos*). Pingree agrees with this and says that Serapio perhaps flourished in the first century B.C. or A.D.[1] However, the collection of definitions that I have translated here was evidently made nearly a millennium later by a Byzantine compiler, perhaps Demophilus.

Some of these definitions are therefore from Serapio, but others are from later writers—for example, Dorotheus and Ptolemy are mentioned. Since the definitions in this tract are from more than one source, there are some repetitions and even some contradictions in the text. Perhaps the compiler

---

[1]See David Pingree, The *Yavanajâtaka of Sphujidhvaja* (Cambridge, Mass. & London, England: Harvard University Press, 1978. 2 vols.), vol. 2, pp. 440-441.

had two or more MSS, from which he made a selection and put together what has come down to us.

In any case, we have here a set of definitions that can be compared with those that are found in Porphyry's *Introduction to the Tetrabiblos*, and in the works of other astrological writers. Some agree and others disagree.

SERAPIO OF ALEXANDRIA
ASTROLOGICAL DEFINITIONS

Effective signs is said of the four *angles* and their *succedents*.

Effective stars are termed those "in power," *angular*, or in **Fortuna**, and those "in phase," or the trigons of the Sun when they occur.

Jointly-effective are those jointly angular, or in **Fortuna**, and those "in phase."

Ineffective are those not so situated.

Helpers are termed those stars that are **receiving** at the same time, or those **bearing witness,** or intervening.

Working together are those in conjunction; while **rendering service** are those throwing themselves together (*sc.,* in aspect).

In concord are those **receiving equally**, with reference to **aspecting in harmony** with each other.

Not in concord are those that are in no way *aspecting* each other, which comes about from the turning away of the *inconjunct* signs.[1]

Inconjunct are those signs that are numbering 6 or 8 signs past each other.[2]

Commanding is termed [a planet] when [it is] in its own house above the earth, angular[3] to **Fortuna**, and [when] the

---

[1]These are planets in *semi-sextile* or *quincunx*—aspects that were not recognized by the classical astrologers.
[2]That is, those that are in what we call *quincunx* aspect.
[3]That is square.

two **Lights** are in aspect; wherefore it is [also] termed **commanding** when it is in its own house angular to a Lot and similarly situated with respect to the Moon. If anyone of the five stars is angular to **Fortuna** [and is] not bearing witness to the Moon, it is effective; if it bears witness to the Moon [by] trine, square, or opposition, it **commands**; if the Sun is in the ASC, it **commands**; even if the Moon [is in] trine to **Fortuna** itself, and the Sun **commands** and is effective.

Dominating are termed those stars that are on the important houses of the geniture, i.e. those that are **angular**, and those "in phase," and those "on the Lots,"[1] and those that are exactly in the conjunctions (*sc.*, New Moons).

A star is **impedited** whenever it is not in suitable [signs], or whenever by chance it is present [with] or surrounded by **malefics**, or opposite [them], or in dexter square [to them]. Because the **benefic** signs (*sc.*, houses) are the ASC, the MC, the 11th, the 5th, [the one called] God (*sc.*, the 9th), [the one called] Goddess (*sc.*, the 3rd). And the **malefic** [signs] are the 2nd, 4th, 6th, 7th, [8th], and the 12th.

Approaching is termed the one that is *following* (*sc.*, in the diurnal rotation) the one *preceding*.

Neighboring is termed a sign that is *succedent* to the Moon towards which it moves; for that one is also called **on the same meridian** (*lit.*, "glued together").

Lying at anchor [is termed] the *sign* that is not even *neighboring* the Moon.

They say it [is] **prepollence by force** whenever a star is on the 9th sign; but whenever none is present on the 9th, it is

---

[1]That is, in conjunction with the Lots.

[not] strong. But they become **prepollent by degrees** in this manner—whenever two stars are present in the same sign, and the one having fewer degrees **prevails** over the one having more degrees, e.g., the star of Mercury in Aries around the 10th degree, that of Saturn in the same sign around the 25th degree—it is evident that the [star] of Mercury **prevails** over that of Saturn *by degrees*.[1]

The stars are said to be **in their own chariots** whenever they are in their own *exaltations*.

Doryphory stars are said to be those that are **oriental** and rise before the Sun. But those rising after the Sun are **occidental**, and [also] those *succedent* to the Moon.

The 15 degrees before the Sun are said to be **pious** because then they are released from the Sun beams; the 15 degrees after the Sun [are said to be] **impious** because the stars found there are less efficacious, having fallen under the Sun beams.

The Moon is said to be in **evening rising** whenever she moves from the new Moon to the full Moon, but in **morning rising** from the full Moon to the new Moon.

Archetypal is said to be the so-called *Part of Fortune*, [and] the four sides of this foundation.[2]

Powerful stars are said to be Saturn, Jupiter, [and] Mars. A **sign** is called **powerful** in each geniture, that is the 10th and the 9th from the Moon, i.e., the **dexter square** and **trine**.

The **first trine** and **square** and **sextile** are said to be the

---

[1]The reason for this is that the one with fewer degrees will rise before the one with more degrees.

[2]Perhaps a reference to a system of houses reckoned from the Part of Fortune.

sinister ones [because] the Moon first joins [herself] to some one of the stars.[1]

On the 10th is termed the **dexter** square.[2]

As soon as the Moon *separates* from the Sun by 15 degrees and *rises*, it is termed **shining**. Similarly too, the stars [with that separation] are termed **shining**.

Of the **succedents**, the 2nd house is **better**; of the four **cadents**, the 6th is **better** because of the trine to the MC.

Whenever **Jupiter & Saturn** are **conjoined in Aquarius**, it is a very troublesome indication for the northern climes, those adjacent to our sea.

The MC to be sure and the individual angles give the **acquisition**, but those in the cadent [houses] declare the **quality** of the acquisition; for example, with Jupiter culminating, and Mars in the 6th, the **acquisition** is from Jupiter, but the **quality** from Mars—for example through military persons. The causing [one is] Jupiter, but the quality [is from] Mars—through that sort of persons.

More powerful are the Malefics in the *cadent* [houses] if any one of them is placed next to an angle, for the causes of the evil are from them, and especially if they are in the 6th. But the ineffective [ones] of the *cadent* stars are the **most inefficacious** in general.

The **Fortune of the Daemon** is often produced, for whenever the **Light of the Sect**[3] is in the terms of [a planet] out of

---

[1]Namely by moving in the sinister direction.

[2]*Cf.* Grant Lewi's "upper square", as defined in his book *Astrology for the Millions* (New York: Doubleday, Doran & Co., 1940; Saint Paul, MN: Llewellyn, 1977 5th ed.), Chapter VI.

[3]The 'conditional luminary'. This is more commonly called the **Light of the Time**.

sect, or not according to masculine or feminine; for example, by day the Sun in a feminine sign, or by night the Moon in a masculine sign; and whenever the **Light of the Sect** is not eastern in the hemisphere of the sect. But if both of the **Lights** [are] in the hemisphere under the earth, and the rest, not in domicile, have [a position] from the prevailing—that is [the] leading **Light**—to the following one, the **Fortune** is understood.

[He says][1] that the **trines are friendlier.** Even if they are *malefic*, they hurt less; but the **squares have the greatest powers**; the **sextiles [are] relaxed**; the **oppositions have rivalries**, but [when they are oppositions] of the Malefics, the evils become more powerful. Moreover, even if they are angular, the conjunctions of the Benefics rejoicing in their own [signs are] *best*, but [when the conjunctions are] of the Malefics, the evils become *milder*.

[He says] that **these oppositions [are] stronger**: Moon in Taurus, Mars in Scorpio; Sun in Leo, Saturn in Aquarius; Jupiter in Cancer, Saturn in Capricorn[2]; because of these gods (*sc.* the Planets) being *in domicile* and their being *in exaltation*, for they become dominant then. But the worst configuration is *by exchange*, and in general by being *opposed* in their own terms, [and] it has the **prepollence** over the one that is exactly opposed. But often the rotundity of the earth hinders and injures the *oppositions*, for example in Virgo/Pisces; however, Jupiter and Saturn are not injured by the rotundity of the earth, and the Moon in Taurus and Mars in Scorpio are not injured, nor are those (*sc.*, Jupiter and Saturn?). But all the others that are in *opposition* cannot be seen by each other because of the rotundity of the earth.

---

[1] Presumably, Serapio.
[2] The text has Jupiter in Capricorn and Saturn in Libra. But this must be a mistake for Jupiter in Cancer and Saturn in Capricorn, so I have corrected it.

[He says] that the [planet], in whose terms the Moon is, is made **House Ruler**[1] whenever by chance the **Ruler of the Terms** [is] in the same sign or degree *aspecting* the Moon. From [those from] which it goes, it makes a *separation*, but to [those] degrees which it *approaches*, it *conjoins* them. But if the **House Ruler** *approaches* the degrees of the terms, and [if] the Moon is with it in the same terms, and if the Moon *conjoins* it, the *conjunction* will be powerful. In just the same manner, if it *separates*, the *separation* will be powerful. But if it is not thus, [and if] it is about to *conjoin* one of the planets either *bodily* or *by aspect* in those degrees which the Moon enters, it is needful to see if the Moon *arrives at* those terms that are those of the star to which she applied by *aspect*, and, if it is so, say [that] she has (dominance). But if by chance the Moon is not about to *arrive at* those terms, that is the same terms of the *aspecting* star, the *conjunction* will not be dominant; but this should be understood [in the case] of *applications*.

[He says] that the Moon **rejoices** conjoining the *solar sect* [when she is] full, or conjoining with *her own sect* [when she is] waning.

[He says] that the Moon, at the time she moves from the **lesser to the medium**,[2] makes those of moderate means; and from the **medium to the lesser**, those with lower [means]; and from the **medium to the greater**, it makes fortunate [persons]; and from the **greater to the medium**, those of moderate means. But these things are *intensified* or slackened according to the **increase of the light**; for when she is **waning**, it is as if it robs her of her power. But the causes of

---

[1]Here, the term **House Ruler** probably means **Ruler of the Nativity**.
[2]These terms refer to the Moon's rate of motion; for example, slow in motion, but accelerating.

good fortune or *disappointment* arise from all these [various] configurations. Unaspected by Jupiter [and] Venus, and **void of course**, she makes moderate [persons] fond of solitude; but, if she is also **waning**, those [who are] disappointed. But it is worse if they[1] are *cadent* or *under the Sun beams.*

The Moon **separating from Mercury** shows habit and purpose; **from Venus**, it makes enjoyment and such like; **from Jupiter**, bereft of one's soul and mind; **from Saturn**, bodily chills and distress in the nerves and some moist disease; but if from the **Sun and Mars**, [it makes] burnings and those things which are generated through fire.[2]

[He says] that he selects the **phases** of the stars in accordance with the [rules of] the divine Ptolemy, and not in accordance with [the rules of] Dorotheus.[3]

[He says] that the stars are **powerful** when they are *square* or *opposite* the Sun, and if they are [not] in ineffective houses.

[He says] that those things that Saturn **benefits**, no other star is able **to take away**.

[He says] that the Moon in *square* or *opposition* to Mars when *full*, and to Saturn when *waning*, and especially in angles, makes *misfortunes* and *banishments.*

[He says] that if any one of the stars chances to be in the **first three degrees of a sign**, it has its power in the previous

---

[1]Which planets is he referring to?

[2]The significations of the Moon's separation from a planet (and applying to none) are given by Firmicus, *Mathesis,* Book 4.

[3]Hence, this sentence cannot be earlier than the 2nd century A.D.; but, since Ptolemy's works were probably not available to the astrological public until the end of the third century at the earliest, it probably dates from the fourth century or later.

sign; just as if any one of the stars chances to be in the **last three degrees of a sign**, it has the power of its denotations in the next sign; and this especially occurs in the case of the Moon and the Sun. If any one is found **on the dividing [line]** of the two signs, it is more powerful and unlimited in its energies.

[He says] that the ASC and the stars **in the orient** and those **in the morning rising** signify those things at the peak of the time of life. And the MC and the [stars in the] **evening rising** and those in the **1st sextile** show the [age of] youth ... The **DSC** and [the stars in] the **western rising** and the †**sextiles** and the **succedents** show the middle [age] ... And [the stars in] the **IMC** and the [stars that are in the] **western rising** and those in the **2nd sextile** and the **succedents** signify the [time of] old age ...[1]

The [stars that are] **under the Sun beams** [are] **weak** ...

Amphoristoi stars are those that are **oriental to the Sun** and **occidental to the ASC**.[2]

[He says] that the stars **rejoice** in *benefic houses* and in those of the same *sect*, for instance in their *own houses*; for then even the Malefics do **good**.

[He says] that the **diurnal stars** rejoice in masculine signs and when oriental to the Sun; and those of the **nocturnal sect** rejoice in feminine signs and when occidental to the Moon.

---

[1]This paragraph is not at all clear and appears to be corrupt.

[2]The Greek word *amphoristoi* is otherwise unattested, but it is related to *amphoreus* 'a jar with two handles, one on each side', so it refers to stars that have a position *on one side* of the Sun and *on the other side* of the Asc. There is no corresponding modern astrological term.

[He says] that the benefics in *malefic houses* and *out of sect* are bad.

[He says] that in *masculine nativities* the stars rejoice when they are in *masculine* signs, but in *feminine nativities* they rejoice when they are in *feminine* signs.

[He says] that the stars are bad[1] when they are opposing their own *domiciles*.

[He says] that in the Division of Times, when we make the progressions of the stars, one must recognize that the *kollêsis* of the planets both with the ASC's and the MC's and with the Lots, [causes] the things that come about for them according to their temperaments to have the effects of being in the MC, especially if they both have the same latitude.[2]

[He says] that first of all, it is necessary to find the Ruler of the Year and its *temperament* and those *aspecting* it, and its *position* according to fixing and according to passage and how it was situated in the nativity.

[He says] that it is also necessary to set up the ASC of the year accurately in the revolution of a nativity and [to note] those aspecting it, and its ruler according to the fixing and according to the passage.

[He says that] the planets rejoice when they are in their own thrones, even if they are *under the Sun beams*, for the benefics increase their good things, and the malefics change into being benefic.

---

[1] This is now called being in detriment.

[2] A *kollêsis* is a conjunction within three degrees. Cumont is suspicious of 'being in the MC', and in fact it is not clear what the author is talking about, unless he means that a close conjunction of two progressed planets in the ASC, the MC, or with a Lot has a 10th house effect.

[He says] that the stars Saturn and Jupiter and Mars **rejoice**, when they are *oriental* and *configured*, but the Moon and Venus when they are *following* and *western*. And Saturn and Jupiter and Mars also **rejoice** when they are configured in the *oriental quarters* of the zodiac, but the Moon and Venus **rejoice** in the *opposite ones*. And the diurnal ...[1]

[He says] that the **ASC** shows the **first age**,[2] and the 12th of the [chart] the things [that happened] before birth; and the 2nd, the latter parts of the first age; and the ASC itself, the middle of the first age; and the **MC** shows the **middle of the whole time of life**; and the 9th, the first parts of the middle; and the 10th, the middle of the middle; and the 11th, the latter parts of the middle; and the **DSC** shows the **last age** of life; but the 6th, the beginnings of the last; and the 7th, the middle of the last; and the 8th, the last of the last, and therefore it is also called [the house of] death. And the **IMC** itself [is called] **death**[3]; and the 3rd of the [chart] the things [that happened] before death; and the 4th itself is death; and the 5th, the things that happened] after death.

[He says] that the astrologers do not approve the prevalence as **chart-ruler** of the one that is *under the Sun beams*, and the *averted* one, and the one that is *out-of-sect*, and the one in its *fall*, and the one in *opposition*—and in a word, the one having a bad *phase*.

[After this, the text breaks off, one leaf
of the MS having fallen out]

---

[1]The rest of this sentence is missing.

[2]Cumont says that Serapio seems to have taken these comments from Hermes Trismegistus's book on the twelve houses. I would add that Hermes related the native's life to the Sun, which begins the day at the ASC, reached mid-day at the MC, and ends the day at the DSC. And the sign that is in the cadent house would have come to the angle first before the sign that is now on the angle, and the sign that is in the succedent house would come to the angle after the sign that is now on the angle.

[3]In other classical writings the IMC is assigned to burial rather than to death.

INDEX OF PERSONS

BIBLIOGRAPHY

Catalogus Codicum Astrologicorum Graecorum (CCAG)
VIII 8.4
  ed. Franz Cumont
  Brussels: Henri Lamertin, 1922.

Lewi, Grant
  Astrology for the Millions (New York: Doubleday,
Doran & Co., 1940)